The Self-Mothering Effect

A Unique Approach to
Childhood Trauma, Narcissistic
Abuse, and Codependency

LadyWake

 Published by: Capucia, LLC
211 Pauline Drive #513
York, PA 17402

Paperback ISBN: 978-1-954920-15-6
eBook ISBN: 978-1-954920-16-3
Library of Congress Control Number: 2021921475

Cover Design: Ranilo Cabo
Layout: Ranilo Cabo
Editor and Proofreader: Janis Hunt Johnson / Ask Janis Editorial
Book Midwife: Carrie Jareed

Printed in the United States of America

Acknowledgments

I would like to thank all the players in my personal game of life. I am so grateful for my family. My girls are the best reasons I could have imagined to fully heal myself; thank you for choosing me. Thank you to the women in my family who endured, who built strength that passed down for generations of survival. I wouldn't be here without you. Thank you, Mom, for the beautiful loving person you are. I am so happy that I could see the true you even through the hardships of life. I must acknowledge my big brother for being a best friend, constant motivator, truth-teller, seeker of justice on my behalf, and all-around amazing brother. Thank you, Leonard. I fully appreciate my village—people who show up for me even when I don't think I need them—my sisters, sistacousin, aunts, cousins, nieces, and girlfriends. Thank you to the host of extended family, friends, and acquaintances who fueled my experiences and helped to create lasting memories. Thank you to my publishing team and the select few friends who encouraged me to the finish line as I shared small pieces of this project. Thank you for the push and for believing in me. Peace and love to you all.

Dedication

This quest to break generational trauma patterns is for my girls—Lily Mtima and Zawati Joy—and the generations to follow. This book is for my nine-year-old self. I love you.

Contents

Introduction

"Tout comprendre c'est tout pardonner."
—To understand all is to forgive all.

There is something to be said about the innocence of a child. As a child I knew who I was, I knew what I wanted. I had no idea how to express that to adults but inside I knew what made me happy. I sat for hours just thinking, daydreaming, and writing stories. I knew even then that I wanted to be a writer. I spent long nights sitting on the floor with my basic desktop computer, with only Word. That was all the computer could do after all, because we didn't have internet. But Word was all I needed because all I wanted to do was write stories. I filled up floppy disk after floppy disk of stories over the years—enough for several books I'm sure. I love to dance so I spent countless hours listening to music and dancing in no specific fashion or order—dancing to a groove that made my heart happy. I knew without a doubt then who I was, and why I was, and what I wanted to offer the world.

1

My life circumstances were what most would consider harsh and unacceptable for a child but somehow it didn't really bother me that much. It didn't start bothering me until other people taught me that there was something wrong with it. It's amazing how children can go through anything with just the most basic of necessities. If there was a warm bed to sleep in, food, and someone to love me I felt okay. My brother was always there to love me, and I always thought my mother loved me too, along with my other siblings. The food was hit and miss but we ate more often than we were hungry. The lights were on more often than they were not. We had soap to wash our bodies and our clothes more often than we did not. I had paper and pencils for school work and school clothes—though not the most expensive or up to date, they still fit. I was content with what I had and who I was and even who my family was. I wasn't comfortable with all the ins and outs of life every day, but I seemed to be content with where it was going.

Now, I didn't really know where it was going but I did know that it was going to get better. I did know that I would get whatever I wanted and that I would be whoever I wanted to be. I did know that I would be different from my surroundings, because I would make different decisions and really aim to be happy. Even when other children teased me and told me I was poor or dirty or ugly, it only hurt for a minute. The pain didn't seem to sink in too deep because I knew in my heart that none of that mattered. I knew in my heart that they had no idea what it was like to be rich, or beautiful, or clean even. I knew they were lashing out because of their feelings of lack. And although I knew I had lack I didn't really feel like I did most days. I didn't feel the need to lash out at others because of my lack, so I just tried to enjoy it all.

The thing that held me back was the fear. It's weird; the fear propelled me to be different but it also kept me from being all that I wanted to be in moment-to-moment living. I feared being taken advantage of or being without my family. And all that I feared came true over time.

My family's struggle hadn't defined me—until outsiders taught me that it should. These issues that I didn't really recognize before as obstacles now became my roadblocks. Now, the struggle that was fighting inside of me laced with hope and expectation became a public struggle. But the expectation was different now. Before, I expected it to all go away at some point. I expected to rise above what I knew and find something new that suited me. Now, people expected me to have hurdle after hurdle to jump over in order to be healthy, to be sane, to be successful. They expected me to be traumatized and live a life similar to my surroundings, just because I was there for so long growing up. They expected me to fight to break the chains and to work hard at being different. I was already different. And though they seemed to notice that, it also seemed like they thought it wouldn't last. It was like my future depended on my effort in every moment to remember my circumstances and to do something that would change them.

I guess that may be true to an extent. It's just that it took so much effort and energy to remember my circumstances.

They wanted me to talk about it and make plans on how to get away. But talking about it made me remember some things I hadn't remembered before. It was like open-heart surgery—reliving trauma over and over again.

I dreamt tirelessly and loved every moment of it but I never remembered them when I woke up. As time went on, knowledge, education, and the system's agenda to open, my eyes to my circumstances wore me down. I could see so much now. And it hurt like hell. I was no longer naïve; I could hear so much now, and I actually understood it as they were relaying it. I could put things together and come to conclusions about what was really happening and what others' intentions were.

I felt stronger. No, I felt powerful. No, I felt on edge! I felt anxious and scared, yet armed and ready.

I'm not sure what I was ready for or what and how I needed to arm myself—but the information made me know that it was time for war. Is war what I really wanted? Can war help me feel free? I didn't feel like I was in a winning situation. Besides, I was a child, and I held no real cards. So one day, I thought: Maybe if I let myself die, I can try it again. It was too overwhelming to fight this fight. Maybe I should just go away and start over and try again.

Well, fear took that away from me, too. I was too afraid to fully go through with it, so I faked it. I faked so much in life now. My happiness had been slowly fading, so I faked it. My understanding had been slowly fading. The more I learned, the less I truly knew, so I faked it. My strength had been at the top of its game when I was five years old, but now that I was fourteen, I had to fake it every day.

Is there such a thing as caring too much? Is there such a thing as knowing too much? I'm not sure if I'm better off knowing or not knowing. The idea that ignorance is bliss is truer than I realized. But now that I'm here, now that I know, how do I *un*know?!

Maybe the answer is not only to know but to move from knowledge into true knowing. That didn't occur to me until many years later—because who knows that their knowledge is not true knowing, when their childlike innocence and knowing has been clouded? The clouding was gradual but very powerful. I now only knew truth when my body shut down, or when my mind shut down and only my body was in control. Is that a thing? I'm not sure if that really happened. I just know that sometimes I would go somewhere else—unsure of how to get back, or how long I was gone, but only sure that it felt better here. I would ask myself: How do I get back there?

I've heard it said that everything happens for a reason. The saying seems to resonate with my soul. But I wonder if it's because I've heard it for so long—or does my inner being really know it to be true? Is there a reason for all the trials and tribulations life has brought thus far? Yes, I guess there would be a reason—but how do I know what that reason is?

After years of wondering, I think I've decided to stop looking for the reasons. I will stop trying to unreel feelings and memories. I will just let them be. I then have to ask myself *how* I will let them be. How do I let go? How do I forget? But do I really need to just forget? I'm not sure if that is actually possible. If I really wanted to, I could reprogram my mind and input new memories to replace the old. What if that could really work? Would it be the right thing to do? Would it be the best thing for me to do? What if it isn't?

What if my memories really do serve a strong purpose? The possibility that it has all happened for a reason that serves me best is still there. It is alive and looming in my face on a daily basis. I try to reason with myself—that I should forget. I mean really forget. Instead, I am less and less bothered by the memories, as I refuse to forget. I refuse to forget. I refuse to forgive. What's the point? Forgiveness is unnecessary when each element of every experience of your life has set you up for success. Who is there to forgive? Shouldn't I say thank-you instead? Shouldn't I recognize the blessings as they are—regardless of how I perceived them when they arrived?

I guess that's the tough thing. The most difficult thing of them all. There is no right and wrong when it comes to reasons. If attraction is all we have, then the individual reasons don't matter. The reason I chose one path versus another means nothing when the outcome is always in my best interest. The reason I attracted one thing versus another means nothing when the experience was always directing me along my best path. But is that the case?

Maybe there is a reason you're reading this book now. My hope is that whatever guided you here will prove worth your while. I hope you gain a new tool, refresh an old one, simply experience shared pain and triumph, or take notice of an idea that resonates with your soul. Grab a journal: This will be an adventure worth noting.

Chapter One

Death of Innocence

"Here this bitch go now," she mumbled. I walked through the door of our third-floor apartment as my mother cursed me. Confused, I looked around the house to see that most things were thrown about. The kitchen and living room areas were technically my chores, so I was responsible for cleaning this huge mess they'd made while I was away. She stood at the kitchen table about fifteen feet away from the door and stared at me with disgust. I don't know what I had done today but her looks really hurt. It was usually her boyfriend Chuck who greeted me with such nastiness, so I was surprised to see her acting this way. I figured Chuck must have had something to do with it though. He always did.

She interrupted my thoughts. She demanded, "Where the fuck have you been?"

"School and work. I'm about to go spend the night at Wanda's house. Remember? You said I could."

She shifted her weight and leaned on the dining room chair. "I didn't say you could do shit, but clean this motherfucking house, bitch."

I wanted to cry. She had never really called me a bitch before today. I'd heard her talk about other people and even to other people like this—but never to me. Never to her eldest daughter.

It was unusually quiet in the apartment tonight. I looked around for clues of my siblings. Finally, I saw one of them stick their little head around the corner in the hallway. I was immediately embarrassed. *They're watching and listening.* My younger sister Nicole was ten years old and my baby brother Lawrence only five. I'd just turned sixteen about three months ago, and as usual, I was concerned for my impressionable siblings. *I don't want them to see or hear this mess.* I scolded them with my eyes to return to their bedroom.

"Oh, so you don't hear me now? Are you fucking deaf? I'm talking to you!"

My eyes returned to her as I sat my backpack on the floor. I didn't know what to do next.

She motioned with her hand. "Bring your ass on over here. Take your shit off. We need to talk."

Following directions, I started with my boots at the door. It was early December in Chicago so the weather was a fright as usual. The winds were high and this day particularly cold for the early part of the winter season. It was about seventeen degrees outside with a wind chill of some ridiculous below-zero temperature. Already on the always-freezing ground was about four inches of snow. My feet were cold in the stylish

Timberland boots I wore to school today. I'd bought them because everyone said they were warm and they were the new style that year for kids my age. I couldn't wait to take them off and put on something warmer. She watched me struggle with my wet boots.

I had risen this morning at 5:30 a.m. to get ready for school. I dressed myself in layers: two pairs of socks, long underwear underneath turtle neck and vest, baggy jeans, hat, scarf, gloves, and a big oversized down coat. I did the same for my two younger siblings and walked them to school—first my little brother, five blocks away, and then my sister, seven blocks from my brother's school but only two blocks from our house. I got on the Green Line train right by Dulles Elementary School on 63rd and King Drive, a school I used to attend with my older brother Leon, which was also attended by my mom and her siblings, now my younger sister's school. That Green Line train took me to downtown Chicago where I switched to the Blue Line train to get to the West Side where I attended Crane High School. I made it just in time for my Academic Decathlon class at 7:30 a.m. before the real school day started at 8:30 a.m.

I was a sophomore, and high school was pretty easy. I was an honor-roll student, well-liked by my classmates and teachers alike. I breezed through the school day and rushed downtown to Ernst and Young where I worked part-time. After work, I walked six blocks to Michigan Avenue and caught the number-three King Drive bus that would drop me off right outside my gated complex. The gate wasn't locked this night so I was fortunate to walk right through and down the courtyard about three hundred feet to my apartment building. The snow hadn't been shoveled and my feet were freezing. It seemed they hadn't warmed up from the walk to the bus after work.

Now my mom was talking again as I unraveled myself from my winter garb. I hung my coat on the chair along with my scarf and sweater. She took a sip of her drink. It was E&J and orange juice, as usual. I could smell it on her breath across the table. I put my battle face on—tried not to look angry or afraid but calm.

She smacked her lips and lit a cigarette. "So, you fucking little boys in the hallway now, huh? Huh? Don't play dumb with me, the neighbors told me all the little nasty shit you've been doing on the stairs. Why you sexing some boy on the stairs? Why not just bring him in the house and fuck like the grown woman you think you are?"

I tried not to make a face but I really wanted to laugh. I was also nervous that she actually might have something on me this time. Did they really see me and the dude in the hallway? I had tried to have sex on the stairs because I obviously couldn't bring him into my mother's house but I had no idea my nosey neighbors were peeking through their peephole watching. Horny bastards were probably getting off on seeing two teenagers trying to have sex. It was a really risky thing, and I knew that.

It had ended up being a waste of my time, anyway. This dude who I liked for years had never really paid me much attention until recently. I had always been the tomboy who hung out with all boys and rarely any girls. I dressed in baggy clothes, wore a different pair of gym shoes every month, and wasn't concerned with having glamorous hair or makeup at all. I was one of the boys, and that's how he saw me. It wasn't until I got a boyfriend this past summer that he started showing interest in me as a possible girlfriend. By then, I had moved on, and learned that he was turning out to be the kind of boy I really didn't want as a boyfriend. But he was fine and I was curious. So on that particular night, I'd allowed him to beg as we talked on my pay-as-you-go flip-phone. He told me about all the things he wanted to do to me and how he was eager to please. I just listened and smiled. I loved to hear men beg; it excited me to be chased like that. Whenever he stopped talking, my only response was, "And what else?"

I'd finally told him he could come over and we could talk some more. He left wherever he was and rang my doorbell about five minutes later. I rushed to the window to see who it was before my mom or Chuck was disturbed. They were locked in their room as usual, and my younger siblings were asleep so I had some alone time. I was in my nightgown because it was almost bed time but I wanted to see him first so I crept out the front door and left the door unlocked while we sat on the stairs and talked. He smelled like weed, which was not surprising these days. I asked silly questions as he made moves to touch and kiss me. We fondled each other for a little while as I watched for signs of my mother or siblings. I tried to sit on his lap and slide his penis in me but he couldn't get hard enough. I got frustrated and ended up sending him home. He left begging and grappling for another chance—when he's not high—but that was rare, and I wasn't a second-chance kind of girl either, so it was a wrap. My neighbors had seen some of that, probably all of that stuff. Why didn't they make some noise or just open the door and say something? Instead of letting me get caught like this.

I responded, "I don't know what you're talking about. Why would I have sex with someone on the stairs? That's nasty."

She sneered, "You're a lying-ass bitch. Why would they lie on you and give me specifics on what you did and who you did it with?"

She had me there. "I don't know. But if they gave you specifics and it was the truth, then you know I didn't have sex—any type of sex. I didn't have oral sex or intercourse with any dude on the hallway stairs." I was extremely frustrated. This was the truth—but only a fraction of it. She didn't need to know that I actually *tried* to have sex on the stairs. Where would that get us right now?

She moved on. "So why is it that the motherfucking DCFS people were knocking on my door today?"

Now I was truly confused. "What are you talking about? What DCFS people? Are you sure it was DCFS?" I hadn't said anything to the Department of Children and Family Services, any counselors or teachers—except that one. My stomach knotted. Did she tell somebody what I've confided in her about? I couldn't breathe all of a sudden.

My mom took that as a sign of guilt. She yelled, "Who have you been telling lies to? You might as well 'fess up now 'cause the truth is out. First, you fucking little boys in hallways like a little whore, then you trying to get my kids taken away from me? I will fucking kill you before I let you take my kids from me. If you want to go, then go. Get the fuck out of here."

"What are you talking about, Ma? I didn't talk to DCFS about anything."

She jumped up from the table. "You a damn liar. They were at my door saying they talked to my daughter and would investigate, whether I let them in or not."

I was dumbfounded. I know I hadn't talked to DCFS, and even the person I did talk to I didn't think would call the authorities because we had a much deeper relationship than pure counseling. "I didn't call DCFS. That would be stupid on my part anyway because I'm still a minor—"

"Don't serve me that bullshit! You've been trying to leave this house forever, so now is your chance."

I started to cry. "I don't want to go to foster care. I've seen my cousins go through the system, and it sucks. Please, I don't want to go!"

She laughed, "I don't give a fuck where you go but you not getting my kids taken away from me."

I didn't know what to say. I tried to think hard about what could've happened. I am pretty confident that my friend, a counselor, hadn't said anything; that would be too risky for her. I hadn't talked to anyone else about home, so how could this be?!

Chuck walked into the room, snickering. "See, I tried to calm Killa down before you got here but she broke loose, I see. Maybe if you try telling the truth she'll go easier on you." He kissed her on the cheek with that stupid toothpick sticking out of his mouth.

She smiled a sly smile and spoke low. "Naw, I'm gon' fuck this bitch up no matter what you say."

He jumped around and beat his fist into his hand, laughing like he was preparing to see the biggest fight of the century. He was so excited.

I was pissed. Standing up abruptly, I walked past them into the back of the apartment—to find my room thrown about and mostly packed up. I looked in my siblings' room, and some of their stuff was packed, too. I started to walk back to the kitchen but Chuck met me in the hallway. He smiled broadly. I walked back into my room to take a closer look. My computer was still on the floor, but my clothes, books, and anything else of mine were packed in boxes and stacked in the center of the room. The closet was covered with hangers, paper, and a few garments thrown here and there. I couldn't believe it. *They are really giving me away to DCFS.* Walking back to the kitchen, I bumped into Chuck, who was refusing to move from my doorway. As I walked into the kitchen he ran up behind me and pushed me in my back. I turned around to hit him but my mom pulled me back by the collar.

"So you just gon' let him put his hands on me and do nothing?"

She rolled her eyes. "Get your shit and let's go."

I tried to get into my winter garb. I put on my boots first, in case I had the opportunity to kick Chuck in the balls. I started to put my sweater on when she grabbed my arm and pulled me toward the door.

"Wait! I'm not dressed!" I screamed.

Chuck pulled my book bag and down coat from the chair and threw them at me. I picked them up off the floor and walked out the door, trying my best to put them on and keep my balance while my mom pushed me down the three flights of stairs. At the bottom of the staircase I stopped and cried out loud.

She yanked me by the coat. "You better not embarrass me in here."

I followed her out the door. *I'm so confused. I don't understand what's just happened. Why are we outside? Where are we going? And, what about all my stuff, which they packed?*

I walked behind her, struggling in the calf-high snow as it was beginning to turn to ice. It was freezing and I didn't even have on the layers I needed to be mildly warm. It seemed like the wind cut right through the thick down coat that covered me. With my arms inside my coat trying to create some heat, I walked a few steps behind her to the gate that led outside the complex.

She abruptly stopped and turned to face me. "You ungrateful bitch! I've been out here selling my ass to take care of you, and you go and try to get my kids taken away from me?!"

My heart instantly sank into my stomach. *I can't believe what I just heard. She has been selling her ass? I don't understand that. Why would she need to sell her ass, when she is a nurse?* She supposedly has a job and works double shifts all the time, and she has a man who lives with us who has a job as well. Plus, I have a job of my own. I bought all my clothes, food, toiletries, and anything else I wanted or needed, including school gym uniforms and fees. I didn't know how serious she was, but the look on her face and my gut told me she was not exaggerating.

I opened my mouth to speak but she smacked me so hard I was sure I felt the flesh leave my face. She pulled me on the other side of the gate and before I could recuperate grabbed me by my scarf, pulling me behind her by the neck. I struggled to keep my balance but I really wanted to sit down and cry for a while. She kept talking but I didn't hear her—just a few cuss words here and there.

She stopped pulling me and asked me why I hadn't responded. I was petrified, in utter confusion and fear. I didn't know what she wanted from me.

She hit me again, this time with a closed fist. I stumbled back and held my own fist back with everything I had. I'm a fighter by nature but I never thought I would feel the need to fight my own mother. I turned to walk in the other direction but she grabbed at my head and pulled my hat off, stomping it into the snow while trying to pull my hair. I tried to cover my face while she beat me upside the head and wherever else she thought it might do damage.

She finally stopped and shoved me in front of her. "Walk, bitch!"

I looked around to find that people were on the other side of the street watching, but nobody said anything. I walked holding my face because I knew I was bleeding. I walked as fast as I could in the high snow, praying that she was done with her fit of rage. We walked in silence for a half block, and then the unimaginable happened. She pushed me in my back and it felt like simultaneously she had picked her foot high off the ground to kick me as hard as she could in the center of my back. I fell on my face and hurried to the fetal position as I realized her foot was coming toward my face. She kicked toward my face but I hid it in my arms. She kicked toward my stomach and I balled up as tight as possible.

I prayed, "Lord, what did I do to deserve this?! My mother is beating me like a stranger on the street. Please save me! Help me, God!"

She stopped and stood looking at me for what seemed like an eternity.

It felt like I was lying on a bed of ice but I was too scared to move. She pulled my hair and ordered me to get up, and I did. Grabbing my arm, she pulled me gently. It was like I had been broken to obey—like when the pimp beats the prostitute to force her obedience, my mom had beaten the fight out of me. I moved with no resistance.

"Let's go," she said. My mom held her hand out and barked, "Give me my money."

Reaching in my pocket, I pulled out the money I had. I put it in her hand.

She sneered at me. "I got that money you were trying to hide from me in your drawer, too. Get the fuck out of here." She walked toward 63rd Street while I shyly lingered by the Walgreens.

I realized I had a change of clothes in my bag, which I forgot I even had for the sleepover. *But I can't go to my friend's house like this. What will I do now? I can't go home either.*

I had asked my mom if I could move in with my cousin about two weeks ago because I couldn't take Chuck's crap anymore. But she'd said no. I was to stay home until I left for college. I said okay and went on with daily life as best I could. My cousin had already agreed to let me live with her before all this so I thought maybe she'd still let me. But now I couldn't find my phone and I hadn't memorized her number. My phone must've gotten lost on the way but I was in too much pain to go back to look for it.

I waited until my mom was out of sight to walk up to the Green Line station. I looked around the platform hoping I didn't see anybody I knew. I did, so I quickly ducked behind the cover wall and hoped that person didn't see me. I needed a phone to get to someone but I didn't know most people's phone numbers. My brother was at my friend's house for the sleepover. I didn't want them to know about any of this.

I felt numb now. I dragged myself to the center of the platform where there is a pay phone, probably the last of its kind in the area. The only person who came to mind was my mentor and counselor, Ms. Kathy. She lived close, had a car, and would probably care enough to come get me and not tell anyone else. I dialed her number from memory.

Chapter Two

Survival Mode

This experience turned into a pivotal story for me right away. In fact, it lingered in the back of my mind and deep in my heart, reminding me that I wasn't enough—and sinking me deep into survival mode. I had been living in survival mode before these events but there was a critical moment in the midst of this particular experience that solidified my path of surviving instead of thriving.

When people speak of *survival* in this way, most understand that it is to endure, or to live through adversity. People survive divorce, failing a test, a health crisis, or a difficult job. These challenges affect people for a period of time, and then they eventually push through to renew their happiness and lust for life. But *living in survival mode* is different. It creates layers of problems, of which most can only see the surface. Instead of time healing all wounds, which allows a person to move forward, it feels more like struggling in quicksand as you sink deeper into depression and hopelessness.

What does it mean to live in survival mode?

"Survival mode" relates to the "fight-or-flight" system of the body—the sympathetic nervous-system response. This happens when the body receives a signal that it is in danger. It then pumps adrenaline throughout the entire body to escape or fight in an effort to keep the body safe and alive. I'm sure you can recall a time when you've experienced an adrenaline rush. Maybe you've been chased by a dog before; you were not sure if it was going to catch you and bite you or not. You might have jumped into action to protect a child or someone you love. Or maybe you even got excited or angry enough to increase your physical strength. These are all useful demonstrations of the sympathetic nervous-system response.

Now, imagine having this response system, as if you were in danger every minute of every day, turned on in perpetuity. How would you feel? What kinds of things would you be driven to do? There might be a better question that sums it up: What happens to the body when there is an excessive or constant amount of adrenaline output?

Our important daily functions get put on hold automatically, while the body anticipates and finds ways to fight the threat. Whether the threat is real and present or not doesn't matter. What matters is that we *think* and *believe* that it is. In our physical experience, our digestion slows, sleep patterns are disrupted, and blood rushes to the extremities—putting stress on the heart, on the other organs, and on the blood vessels. In return, we suffer constant headaches, higher risks of heart attack and stroke, blood clots, insomnia, anxiety, and paranoia.

What drives people into survival mode?

The answer is fairly simple: trauma. Trauma is not as simple as something unwanted or uncomfortable happening in your life. Trauma is created from life-altering experiences. They might not all feel life-altering at the time, but if an experience creates a deep emotional or even physical wound, it is trauma. Traumas come in many forms but for the purpose of understanding survival mode we will focus on mental and emotional trauma. When trauma is experienced in childhood, it is proven that those traumatic experiences create an interruption in brain development. This does not necessarily mean the child will be a slow learner or anything of that sort. But it does mean that the child will lock up and function mainly with his or her sympathetic nervous system. It means that the child will live in a constant state of fear.

My state of survival mode started early in my childhood, as I saw nothing but lack around me. My neighborhood was full of people in pain, people afraid of anything different yet in total disgust over their lives and anyone who was like them. I felt like I didn't have any family because my mom was in and out; and my siblings and I were no longer allowed to be around extended family for fear of spilling household secrets. There were times when we didn't have food, or lights, or clothes and shoes that fit. I fought boys almost daily because they always tried to touch me. Worse, I was constantly afraid of being raped in my home since my mom's boyfriend was a child predator. There was no surprise when I finally noticed as an adult that I had PTSD (Post-Traumatic Stress Disorder)—

21

WHEN TRAUMA IS EXPERIENCED IN CHILDHOOD, IT IS PROVEN THAT THOSE TRAUMATIC EXPERIENCES CREATE AN INTERRUPTION IN BRAIN DEVELOPMENT.

which stemmed from living with my sympathetic nervous system constantly turned on.

My childhood environment is a scenario that gives us a small peek at what can happen when an adult has an excessive amount of adrenaline in the body. For a child, before the body is worn down by constant adrenaline, the results are more internal. Children operating in fight-or-flight mode will do just that: fight others physically or verbally, or fight against anything an adult tells them to do. Or, they might operate mostly in flight—where they run or retreat inwards from anything that makes them feel vulnerable or seen.

Flight was my main method of survival. I was an intelligent kid who was highly involved in school and home life with friends and siblings. But I was hiding daily. I didn't show who I really was but put on a strong mask so people could see only what I wanted them to see. I was in pain, scared and unsure of myself every day, but I acted like I was the toughest most confident girl in the school. The faking did help me get things done and meet goals that I had set for myself. But it also played a major role in ingraining those practices into my being so that I eventually completely lost who I really was.

Survival-mode habits

By the time I went to college at the age of seventeen, I had established these habits from surviving my childhood. On the surface, it looked like I had survived and made it out of the stressful circumstances unscathed; but on the inside I knew something wasn't right. The measure of survival was set by those around me—friends, teachers, and other family members. I wanted the look of physical survival as well. I wanted to leave the projects, to graduate college, and to be able to take care of myself without government assistance. But underneath all of that, what I really wanted was to be happy.

I had set and completed many goals within a short time frame because I thought those things and places would make me happy. The problem was, I didn't really know how true happiness feels. After all, I learned happiness by watching other people around me who claimed they were happy. They weren't. They were in fact faking it, just like me. Growing up in my neighborhood left its residents feeling unworthy, gutless, and afraid on many levels. It made sense that people would lie about being happy with their life, when they felt powerless to change it. Their unhappiness played out in many ways—mostly in how much and how often they consumed drugs and alcohol to alter their state; how much they fought each other and complained about being broke; how much stress they felt and expressed on a daily basis; and how their relationships either didn't work out altogether or made them miserable, yet they stayed in them out of duty and to keep up appearances.

Many people feel that their survival-mode habits are what's best for them. Are they, though? Does survival mode serve us as women, sisters, mothers, daughters, and partners? No! In fact, it breaks down our femininity in devastating ways. We are no longer able to be as open and as nurturing as we need to be to care for our children and other loved ones. Over time, our genes are covered in these new habitual signals that tell us to fight or run and hide. This means that survival mode is passed down to the next generation.

We are also then unable to meet the masculine as the strong feminine partner they need. Instead, we show up as more masculine most of the time. Don't get me wrong; everyone has both masculine and feminine energy. But, if a man is mostly masculine in search of a woman to care for, he needs the feminine to match his energy. A yin-and-yang approach, so to speak. The masculine is the protector by nature; but the woman in survival mode shows up as her own protector, thus stripping the masculine person of his job. If the masculine man does not feel needed he will feel defeated before the game has begun. These mixed-up mismatched energetic relationships are a strain on both parties.

I am not letting men off the hook. Men have massive responsibility in making families work and stay together; but women have equal responsibility in their own unique way. I speak mostly to women because I know we are the first point of contact for a new person born into this world. When a child is *in utero* it is already gaining from the woman carrying. This means that the child is receiving its first lessons energetically and hormonally, causing early tendencies to form straight from the parents' DNA as well as from the mom's physical and emotional habits. Constant "survivors" originate from the toxic stress experienced by our young children even from the early stages in the womb.

This knowing is already a huge deal for women as individuals and for our families. Imagine if we became super-aware of our pivotal stories and survival-mode habits that followed—how that would impact the world. Women rule the world. Yes, I said it. We are on the front lines of bonding

IMAGINE IF WE BECAME SUPER-AWARE OF OUR PIVOTAL STORIES AND SURVIVAL-MODE HABITS THAT FOLLOWED— HOW THAT WOULD IMPACT THE WORLD.

WE ARE ON THE FRONT LINES OF BONDING WITH OUR CHILDREN, AND THUS WE SHOULD BE ON THE FRONT LINES OF TRUE EMOTIONAL HEALING AND MASTERY.

with our children, and thus we should be on the front lines of true emotional healing and mastery. In this way, we can reduce significantly our children's susceptibility to stress, and to emotional pain and trauma. We can create a ripple effect that will eventually heal entire generations of families. Imagine how this massive healing would serve us as a society!

Recognizing the effects of survival mode

Sometimes we know that something is wrong but we are not quite sure what it is, or what to do about it. We even go to counseling, seek religious help, dive into our work, or lose ourselves in our children. All the while, we hide the events leading up to survival mode—saying things to ourselves like, "I survived, so I don't have to think about those things anymore."

In this space of uncertainty, we don't realize how living in survival mode affects our lives in relationships, business, physical image, and mental/emotional health. It is the hiding that kills us. It is one thing to experience trauma, acknowledge it as it is, and make moves to heal. It is an altogether different thing to experience trauma and pretend it didn't happen while watching people you love and countless others around the world experience the same trauma and try to hide it as well. People like to think that they are unique in their problems; but as human beings, we all have the same basic problems. We also have the same basic needs. If we meet our basic needs, then we have an actual chance of real survival, which comes with healing those deep wounds.

We may know cognitively but we never really linked those events to the automatic response we give in life. How can we become more aware of our automatic response to life? First, we must make the decision to see our circumstances and experiences as they truly are. For many, this vulnerability will mean reliving or feeling the pain of the truth for the first time. That's okay. We have pain and fear as an emotional signal to pay attention—and perhaps, change something. We need to be aware of our pain signatures and where they come from. What's more is to be aware of the underlying issues on a foundational level.

It seemed like my childhood experiences created the feelings of anxiety, panic, and shame in my early adulthood, but nobody could help me understand why. What was the real reason that these experiences caused such a deep-rooted response in me?

We now know that the side effects of adversity are rooted in biology. Early adversity in childhood has been proven to alter biology—the immune system—and to make these individuals more susceptible to abuse and illness. As I've stated, when children are traumatized, it can cause dysfunction through an interruption of their brain development. This means that the child will get caught in survival mode earlier and faster. When trauma happens, the child's brain will activate the fight-or-flight response mode, but because the child's development is interrupted by severe or constant trauma, the child can get stuck in this autonomous nervous system response—and thus stuck in survival mode. This makes it very difficult for these children—and these same people when they become adults—to control their emotions, regulate their stress, and have awareness of situations with covert danger, like mental and emotional abuse.

I am a prime example, as I had effectively run away from one abusive and traumatic environment smack into another one...over and over again. Later in life, I realized how these experiences had affected my ability to trust. In fact, I had learned no reason to trust because I had no major experiences to pull from. There was some consistency with my brother Leon but after he was kicked out of the house at sixteen, I was alone and had to rely on my own strength to survive. Maybe more important, I didn't see it. I was completely unaware of the seriousness of my circumstances and experience. I knew that many things happening to me weren't okay, but thought I was "woman enough" to handle them. I was a girl acting like a woman because I felt I had no choice if I wanted to survive.

It was not okay, but I had so much adversity in my early childhood that I was not only numb but also unaware of how healthy love looked and felt. On top of my lack of awareness, I was fiercely private, hiding in my shame so that nobody had a chance to help me. This created a cycle of toxic love, and shaped my ideas about love. I thought I had to be the one to give everything and play the martyr in order to be loved. To be loved is a basic human need, which means that even in survival mode we will do what we think it takes to feel loved.

In my early adult life I spent many years in counseling trying to unpack all of my feelings and fears. It was there that I realized I had not been aware of most happenings in my life. I was walking around like a zombie getting through the days. I had accomplished many of my goals around education and career, but my personal relationships were shallow or nonexistent. When I began to allow myself to be aware of my experiences and of the way they made me feel and think, it was excruciating. I would try to feel it but then I would run and hide again, as that was the safest thing to do. These were mostly mental/emotional response symptoms of trauma in childhood; but there are also physical and psychological symptoms that are being studied more extensively in the medical community. As it turns out, there is a potentially large, negative physical impact that can accompany survival mode.

Adverse Childhood Experiences (ACEs)

A study of Adverse Childhood Experiences (ACEs) took a deeper look at the symptoms of survival mode. Experts assessed about 10,000 adults who had experienced some kind of childhood abuse/trauma or household dysfunction. They took all of the different types of trauma and dysfunction and divided them into seven categories. Those categories were: living with someone who was a substance abuser; violence against the mother; family member mentally ill or suicidal; family member imprisoned at any point; or psychological, physical, or sexual abuse. They then compared these categories of ACEs to certain measures of adult health status, disease, and adult risk behavior. More than half of the respondents reported at least one, and one-fourth reported two or more categories of childhood exposures. The researchers found a graded relationship between the number of categories of childhood exposure and each of the adult health-risk behaviors and diseases studied.

Persons who had experienced four or more categories of childhood exposure—compared to those who had experienced none—had four- to twelve-fold increased health risks for alcoholism, drug abuse, depression, and suicide attempts; a two- to four-fold increase in smoking, poor self-rated health, fifty or more sexual intercourse partners, and sexually transmitted disease; and a 1.4- to 1.6-fold increase in physical inactivity and severe obesity. The study concluded that there is a strong relationship between the breadth of exposure to abuse or household dysfunction during childhood and multiple risk factors for several of the leading causes of death in adults.

What does this mean for the average person? We know in general that if you have experienced some kind of trauma in your life, you will deal with mental and emotional side effects. If you've experienced one type of trauma, then you are at a higher risk of living with one of the leading causes of death in adults. If you experienced four or more types of trauma, the numbers grow exponentially. Let's say you saw your mom abused once; your uncle went to jail when you were a kid; your cousin was deemed mentally ill; and your father verbally abused you a few times. These experiences don't seem very traumatizing on the surface. But if they were your childhood experiences, this study says that you are now *four to twelve times more likely* to deal with addiction, depression, being overweight, and/or feeling generally unhappy—or even attempting suicide. Wow. That compounding effect is impactful!

You may have heard of compound interest or other matters dealing with finance, but compounding works in other areas of your life as well. You can create a compound effect with most things. If you make small incremental changes to your diet, for example, eventually you will see large changes in the health of your body and weight. Whether that change is up or down depends on what you're eating. Either way, the change won't be immediate but will happen over time; and when it does happen it will feel like a large change considering those small consistent actions. Physical exercise is another example. If you exercise a small amount several days a week you won't see the benefit immediately. In fact, you might think you're not doing much at all. But over time others notice that you've leaned out or built muscle, and they'll start to compliment you on your progress. It is then that you realize that your small workouts have paid off way more powerfully than you thought was possible.

Even if you feel your experiences were minor or nowhere near as intense as mine, you are still at risk of trauma side-effects that are mental, emotional, and physical, along with facing the danger of living in survival mode. Conversely, if you feel that the trauma you've endured was equally or even more intense than my examples here, you now know for certain that you have many trauma side-effects to overcome. You also know that you are probably right now living in survival mode.

Your awareness is incredibly important to your healing.

Awareness Assistance

Going forward, we're going to attend what I call "AA" together—that is, Awareness Assistance. AA is a conscious opening of the mind and heart regardless of the pain it may cause, so that we might become more aware of ours

Awareness Assistance must be a combination of revealing the truth so that it can be seen and understood, while rebuilding the psyche with an interruption of patterns.

It's like having a personal coach. If you routinely get sad or give up after remembering how you've failed in the past, AA is a coach who will step up and give you perspective. The coach will remind you of things you learned in those last experiences and push you to make a different decision this time—right away. It's hands on. And I've learned over time that you can do it for yourself as well. At this point, if you haven't already, it would be beneficial for you to grab a journal and begin tracking your thoughts and feelings as you journey through this book.

~

We give ourselves assistance to our awareness by asking essential questions. Let's give it a try now by answering these questions in your journal:

- Ask yourself point blank: "What happened to cause *my fear of mom* my trauma?" Think it through and write down any pivotal stories that you have.
- What happened to make you feel less than worthy, or afraid of your own voice? *moms rejection*
- When did this event happen? *0 - entire life*
- Write down the details of what you remember. What were you thinking and saying to yourself

or others? What decisions did you make in that moment that shaped your life moving forward—for better or worse?

- You might have more than one story that helped to shape your particular mode of survival; is there one that stood out from the rest? Was it because of the severity, or the length of time? What was the unique way that it affected you?

I laid out a very detailed example in Chapter One of this book. Feel free to model it to encompass as much detail as possible from your own experience. As we move along, you will see more and more how my pivotal stories took me on a journey of survival—a hero's journey with high levels of pain and tough lessons, so that I could transcend them and gain wisdom—for myself, for my family, and for you.

Chapter Three

The WAAKE Healing
Methodology

The night my mom put me out, Ms. Kathy picked me up from the train station. She took me to her apartment in Hyde Park and wrapped me in blankets. My mind went on a frightened trip as Ms. Kathy held me tight and rocked. I had told her some of the story on the ride to her house but I was too shaken up to share many details. She was patient. It seemed like Ms. Kathy was always patient. I cried as she cleaned my face. I welcomed the alcohol sting on my wounds.

I can easily recall the first time I actually let Ms. Kathy into my world. I had just had a fairly traumatic experience, and she just happened to be there, asking me questions about my life and ensuring me that she was trustworthy. That day, I decided to test her promises and tell her exactly what had happened. Plus, I was scared and ashamed and really wanted an adult to understand me. I sat in the tiny counseling room with the door closed and let these thoughts swirl in my head for the entire third class period while Ms. Kathy looked at me intently. She asked question after question as if she knew I had something significant to say. I should've been in class but would be excused since I was in the counselor's office.

As the bell rang for fourth period I let out a long sigh and finally started to speak. "I can't say it but I wrote it down in first period. You can read it if you want."

Ms. Kathy perked up from her laid-back position in her office chair and watched me fumble through my notebook. I flipped past a dozen stories and journal entries, holding the notebook close to my body. When I finally handed it to her, Ms. Kathy seemed shocked. She reached out slowly with her mouth wide open. "Did you write all of this? Do you write every day? This is amazing."

I snatched my hand back as quickly as I could. "I don't want to share this stuff. Only this page that I'm showing you." She shook her head fiercely. "No problem. I won't pry."

I handed her the page I wanted her to see and she began to read aloud:

The winter time brought about scarce streets and barely lit mornings for the 6:30 a.m. bus pickup for school. I was in 8th grade and still riding the school bus. Leon had already transitioned to 9th grade so the school bus was no longer an option for him. He used to accompany me through this process but now I was alone. I had no deep feelings about riding the bus since I had done it a hundred times the year before. I already knew most of the kids who would be riding the bus this year. What I didn't know was how weird it would feel waiting at the bus stop alone. As the cold weather hit strong in early November, the bus stop became a lonely place.

I stood alone one early morning watching random stragglers pass on the opposite side of the street when I noticed a man pacing at the corner of the block. He paced about 10 feet back and forth disappearing on the side of the building and then returning to the corner of the block. I figured maybe he was waiting for the bus as well but trying to keep warm in the meantime as most Chicagoans did by moving around at the bus stop. But something in me also flashed red flags and caused me to look around for other people close enough to see me. I walked out a few paces from the wall I was leaning on in an effort to be seen by cars and anyone passing by.

The man stopped pacing. He stood at the end of the block about 50 feet away from me and looked in the opposite direction like he was looking for the bus or waiting on a ride. After a few seconds he walked away down the perpendicular block. I exhaled and continued to wait on the bus. I was standing midway between the actual bus stop and the end of the street so as not to interrupt the CTA bus when my school bus arrived. I waited another five minutes before a woman joined me at the bus stop. Relieved to have her there, I ignored the man when he came back to the corner but this time he did not ignore me. His head sunk into his coat. He wore a skull cap pulled down close to eyes. I quickly assessed his tattered jeans and run-over sneakers as he walked slowly towards me. "Is he a crackhead?!" I wondered to myself.

I stepped back out of the center of the walkway and a little closer to the lady as he approached me. I wasn't scared of him but I had no idea why he would be approaching a little girl at the bus stop early in the morning. He walked up to me and I studied his face in case I needed to recall it later. He was probably six feet tall with smooth light brown skin. His curly mustache sat awkwardly above his thin lips. I breathed deeply and put on the meanest face possible as I looked into his eyes. He seemed very confident but also kind of aloof. He didn't seem to even notice the lady standing next to me. That made me uncomfortable so I glanced at the lady to gauge her reaction. She was minding her own business.

I quickly put my hand inside my coat sleeve and retrieved the knife hidden in the secret pocket inside my coat. I brought my hand down to my side gripping the knife hard as weird mystery man pulled his hand out of his pocket and revealed to me a condom with a fifty-dollar bill sitting on top of it. I was stunned. I had never experienced such a thing and had no idea what to do. Yet, for a split second, I thought about it. Why did I think about it?! I thought about the oversized dingy clothes I currently wore and the many sneakers I switched in and out of every few days that never fit and belonged to my mother's boyfriend. I wanted to work but was too young for anyone to feel comfortable hiring me. I never even had enough money to go on a simple field trip with my class. I had no gym uniform or ID because my school fees weren't paid, and I could forget school pictures as well. I glanced at the lady again who seemed shocked as well but she still minded her own business.

I carefully made the knife more visible as I shook my head no. He walked away. The man looked back a couple of times. I wondered if he could read my mind or something. I made a firm mental note to tell my brother about this later so I wouldn't have to stand on the bus stop alone anymore. Leon would surely protect me.

My school bus finally arrived and I jumped on with the persona of the coolest kid in school murmuring "what's up?" to the few early riders. They instantly looked me up and down to assess my designer clothes and name-brand shoes. I sported some trendy air max sneakers with baggy jeans and shirt consistent with the typical tomboy style of the 90s. My oversized down coat and skull cap I thought made me look more like a boy than a girl, but it kept me warm so I wore them proudly. After a couple of nonverbal approvals, I found a seat and looked out the window pretending my life was different. I imagined that I would tell my mom after school and she would start walking me to the bus stop or driving me to school herself. Mom was usually gone by the time I left home in the morning and scarcely around in the evening to talk to about anything but I fantasized anyway….

If you had asked me then, I would've said I was a well-adjusted teen who was book smart and street smart. I didn't acknowledge the fact that I carried a knife around everywhere I went. I knew how to use it. I had it easily accessible and was prepared to defend myself. I didn't trust anyone and mostly kept to myself. I definitely didn't trust men, as I had learned from adults and my own experiences that men were predators of women.

This experience spoke loudly of my childhood wiring.

Transforming trauma into power

We've talked briefly about "AA"—Awareness Assistance—and the important role it plays in healing. Now, I want to fully introduce you to the WAAKE Healing Methodology of transforming trauma into power. This methodology was born out of the biggest fight of my life thus far. That was the fight for my mental/emotional freedom from a covert narcissist. I will tell you about that experience in the coming chapters. First, allow me to familiarize you with the acronym WAAKE.

W	**Wiring** – How you are wired or trained to think, see, understand, and respond.	
AA	**Awareness Assistance** – Turning triggers into power aids instead of trauma reminders.	
K	**Knowing** – Turning knowledge to knowing by combining it with learned wisdom. This creates your foundational belief system and ideals.	
E	**Esteem** – Consistent building and defending your rising self-esteem and self-love.	

The WAAKE Healing Methodology first helped me to overcome narcissistic trauma and self-love deficits, and to transform my trauma into personal power. Then, I went on to teach numerous women how to transform their own trauma using this self-mothering methodology. It has served me and others in a major way.

I formulated the WAAKE Healing Methodology after fully understanding, living, and then healing the six tenets of survival mode. These tenets make up the toxic relationships and experiences a person in survival mode is likely to struggle with. These harsh experiences are only amplified by the ACEs that were manifested in childhood. The story you just read is a good example of wiring. Now, allow me to help you better understand how the tenets of survival mode come into play.

I've grouped survival mode into six tenets based on the commonality I've found in the experiences of people living in survival mode. In this story, I demonstrated three of the six. These tenets reside deep within our psyche—and even in our body. If you think back to an experience that felt traumatic to you, you'll notice that you not only remember the details in your mind but your body tends to respond as if you are back in that traumatic moment. The same thing goes when you are thinking about something that was impactful in a positive way. An easy example is particularly exceptional lovemaking. When you make love in an exceptional way and think back on it, your entire body helps you to feel the experience. The thoughts and feelings combined are what make it so difficult to change habits and set identities.

IF YOU THINK BACK TO
AN EXPERIENCE THAT
FELT TRAUMATIC TO YOU,
YOU'LL NOTICE THAT YOU
NOT ONLY REMEMBER
THE DETAILS IN YOUR
MIND BUT YOUR BODY
TENDS TO RESPOND AS IF
YOU ARE BACK IN THAT
TRAUMATIC MOMENT.

Let's look at the six tenets of survival mode:

1. Looking for Danger – In survival mode, one is always expecting danger to arrive at any moment. That is in fact why we ran or fought in the first place. Since we are stuck in that fight-or-flight response system when living in survival mode, our main focus is to prepare—to look for what might potentially harm us. This makes us extremely selfish. We live as if we are always fighting for our very life.

2. Shame (Quiet or Loud) – Shame is a major way to seal someone into survival mode. Shame is the main recipe in creating a sense of low self-worth in another or in oneself. There is a *quiet shame*—where people hold all the feelings of doubt and unworthiness inside while they put on a smiling face for the world. Then there is *loud shame*—where individuals will outwardly shame everyone else for the thing they are most ashamed of. This makes them feel like they are fooling others and thus hiding their shame the best.

3. Guilt – Guilt is a close cousin of shame in that it deeply enforces the ideas of unworthiness and victimhood. When someone is feeling guilty in survival mode, it creates a kind of worm hole of negative feelings. Failed responsibility and regret turn into more selfishness, shame, and often anger. The guilty party is often unsure if they should feel guilty, because after all, someone did something to them first. Unfortunately that truth doesn't make the guilt go away and so the cycle continues.

4. Victim – Feeling like a victim ties closely with guilt. Nobody likes to feel guilty about anything. If you are living in a constant state of guilt it is a direct attack on your well-being. The mind is conditioned to help us survive; but guilt leads down a rabbit hole of depression and suicidal ideation for most people. Knowing the danger of this rabbit hole, the brain helps us find people to blame for our feelings. We become victims of our circumstances and of other people's judgments and deeds. Victimhood is safer and ideally keeps us alive longer than the shame-and-guilt duo.

5. Running – This is the kind of running that makes a person noncommittal. You've met someone with commitment issues—either by their own admittance or by your assessment. These individuals are always looking for something better to make them feel better. They don't trust themselves to make decisions so they think there is always something or someone better out there—that they might be missing out.

6. Codependency –"Birds of a feather flock together" is a popular saying to enforce the idea that people connect with others who are like themselves. History, the Law of Attraction, and countless studies have confirmed that this is the case. If a person is in survival mode and dealing with the tenets described above, they are ripe for a good old-fashioned trauma bonding. Codependency is an unhealthy psychological reliance of one person on another. It is an attachment rooted in addiction. Each person is addicted to the other in some way, and they rely on that bond to keep their spirits up. Codependency is also living in complacency, which is why it never creates the happiness and fulfillment each party is searching for.

⁓

- Which tenets of survival mode can you identify in your main pivotal story?
- How do those tenets play out in your life right now?
- Which tenet of survival mode drives you the most?

These tenets of survival mode are symptoms of a major underlying problem. WAAKE gives us an opportunity to address the real problem causing survival mode symptoms. In this story, we see a vivid example of how my wiring created a space of defensiveness and distrust, along with a need for approval and protection all at the same time. I was presenting as a victim and living in survival mode before I knew much about life in general.

Remember that wiring is how you were taught to think, see, understand, and respond. The sad—and simultaneously empowering—truth is that you must first become aware of your wiring if you are going to be able to do anything about it.

Awareness is the foundation for change. Unfortunately, self-awareness isn't easy without some clear failures, upsets, and pain in life experiences. Of course we can be taught self-awareness at a young age, and avoid lots of pain along our

THESE TENETS OF
SURVIVAL MODE ARE
SYMPTOMS OF A MAJOR
UNDERLYING PROBLEM.
WAAKE GIVES US AN
OPPORTUNITY TO
ADDRESS THE REAL
PROBLEM CAUSING
SURVIVAL MODE
SYMPTOMS.

journey. But those who have experienced trauma—which has left them pushing through life in survival mode—are usually not very self-aware of their wiring.

There's a saying, "experience is the best teacher." This rings true in life, in career, in relationships, and in many other ways as we journey through our lives. Experience is incredibly powerful in its lessons and staying power. I still don't know of a better way to truly learn.

But there is good news: You don't have to experience everything for yourself to get the lessons. You can tap into understanding your own wiring so that you know what experiences might serve you in a certain stage of life.

The human brain is incredibly complex—a genius all on its own. If you ask yourself specific questions, your brain will find a way to get the answers to you. Your brain will literally light up and release serotonin, allowing it to more easily find answers and create solutions. In this case, it helps to ask questions of yourself to help you see where you stand, why you think the way you do, what triggers you, and much more. One way to know more about your wiring is to begin understanding your usual set point.

What is a set point?

A set point is the preferred level of functioning. It works much like how a thermostat is set to a specific temperature: As the air in the room fluctuates, the thermostat's temperature reading might go up or down but the device always works to get back to its set temperature. Human beings also function like this. We have a mental/emotional set point that drives our behavior, thoughts, beliefs, and responses. Life might introduce experiences that take us higher or lower on the emotional scale but we always work to get back to our set point—which is also our personal standard of being.

How to address wiring that isn't serving you in a positive way

After you become aware of your wiring or your set point, you can begin to rewire your brain or reprogram your mind. Your newfound awareness opens the door for change. I tried to reprogram my mind with a variety of popular tactics. I used affirmations, mindfulness exercises learned in therapy, prayer, meditation, crystals, and more. I worked at it for years, feeling like I was progressing for brief time periods only to find myself back in depression and feeling lost. I was working hard but the results weren't lasting.

I had begun to understand my wiring but every time I tried to move past it, I had to battle with the trauma that lived in my body and in my biology. Triggers would show up and I always had a trauma response instead of a balanced, grounded, healed response. This is when I further started to understand how deeply impactful wiring is, and also that I needed something different if I were ever going to break free from my trauma. This bigger understanding led me to a new search for how to control my triggers and trauma responses through Awareness Assistance.

You must begin wherever you are. Before I knew about Awareness Assistance, I had only minimal knowledge of my wiring. And that's where I started. As you go through your day, ask yourself questions and relax while the answers come. Let me be clear; you *will* receive the answers to your questions. This is a definite. The details might come in the form of life experiences, or as a whisper in your head—but your questions *will* be answered in any case.

∿

- Ask yourself: What do I believe about myself?
- What do I believe about other people?
- Why did I respond with [insert negative emotion] to this [insert specific incident] experience?
- How can I love myself more today?

These are important questions that will help you to get to know yourself better and therefore to get the healing process started.

Chapter Four

Assisting Your Own Awareness

elf-mothering is much like how it sounds. To *mother* is to nurture through caring, protection, and creation. We are all mothered to some extent, as we are all born from a mother's womb. In the womb we learn about the world from our mother's perspective. We eat what she eats and even feel her emotions. Once outside of the womb, mothering is done intentionally or haphazardly but we all learn—from our mothering or lack thereof—how to survive, how to get along, and what to believe.

Self-mothering really begins with an understanding of your own wiring. But this isn't enough. We must then move into Awareness Assistance and use it as a tool for healing.

As adults it is possible to mother ourselves out of old wiring and trauma into a new way of thinking, believing, and response. We use similar tactics as our mothers used to teach us new things and establish a solid foundation of who we intend to be. But it is more difficult as an adult because we must first *un*learn a lot of our wiring or training from childhood.

AS ADULTS IT
IS POSSIBLE TO
MOTHER OURSELVES
OUT OF OLD WIRING
AND TRAUMA
INTO A NEW WAY
OF THINKING,
BELIEVING, AND
RESPONSE.

Awareness Assistance stands as the core of transforming our brain and body and turning trauma into power.

Before we get into how you can assist your own awareness, allow me to share with you how I came to understand the importance of awareness. I was living in "ignorant bliss"—which was anything but blissful—when life took a series of turns and showed me what I really wanted in life at that time.

Traumatic bonding

I had a major trauma-bonding experience with Ms. Kathy. Of course, I did not realize it at the time. Traumatic bonding occurs because of ongoing cycles of abuse where there is a powerful reward-and-punishment system that creates an intense emotional bond. Counseling sessions in the little computer room in her office helped me to trust her over time. She asked the same types of questions over and over and I avoided them or sat quietly staring at her, not sure if I should tell her the truth. I wanted to tell her the truth but I was afraid of the possible consequences. I didn't want to get my mom in trouble and I definitely didn't want to have my family broken up. But I wanted to tell the truth. I wanted someone to know how much pain I was feeling on a daily basis. I wanted help with figuring things out. I wanted to save my family.

I kept going back to the office and hanging out. I would help her with whatever she allowed and ask her questions about all sorts of things. She would tell me stories of experiences and places to visit around the U.S. and the world. I thought she was the smartest woman in the building sometimes. She seemed so classy. I listened to her conversations with other students and staff and learned what she liked and disliked.

I noticed all of this before I was officially in her program. My brother was one year older and started her program before I was allowed to do so. I followed him around and learned a lot about the program and Ms. Kathy. Kids would hang out with Ms. Kathy after school and on the weekends. I saw that she had a group of students who loved her and trusted her completely. She would give students a ride home sometimes or gather a small group and take them to dinner at a nice restaurant.

I remember the first time she gave us a ride home. My brother Leon and I had gone to dinner with Ms. Kathy and two other students that evening. She took each of us home, dropping off Leon and me last since we lived closest to her house. I was intrigued with how much she seemed to know about food and the finer things in life.

After that night, Ms. Kathy started to hang out with us on a more regular basis. The next year when I was in her program Ms. Kathy spent a lot more time with me one on one. We did all the same things inside the counselor's office and more after school. I would stay late with her some days and she would take me home. My brother had a job already so he would leave school earlier, leaving me to travel home alone.

One late afternoon I was helping Ms. Kathy with some paperwork in her office. She talked to me about my future and her belief in my success. I walked to her as she sat at her desk and kissed her cheek quickly. I dipped out of sight fast so as not to see her response or to show anymore of my feelings. That kiss turned into regular kisses on the cheek both ways. We evolved to goodbye kisses after a ride home. Then one day I found myself sitting in Ms. Kathy's car outside the gate of my community, down the street from my apartment building, holding hands and talking. I would cry about something that made me sad or embarrassed and she would hold my hand and talk me through the tears. This made me feel so safe.

I trusted Ms. Kathy more and more, and thus opened up to her more and more about my life outside of school. After I got a job we spent more time doing things like this. She would invite me to her house for dinner and tea or wine. I had my first drinks of cider and wine with Ms. Kathy. I loved that she treated me like an adult sometimes. We would watch movies and talk in the candle light but I mostly just wanted to sleep on her couch. I was always exhausted, and her house felt comfortable and safe. I took advantage of any time I could get away from my house to spend with Ms. Kathy hanging out or sleeping on her couch. I would lay in her lap and tell her my stories or listen to her tell her stories. She rubbed my hair and kissed my forehead every once in awhile. I never felt uncomfortable or like we had an inappropriate relationship. I thought she was my angel sent to rescue me from life in the hood. I wanted a different life. And the more I learned about hers the more I thought I might like that kind of life.

Then, a cool fall evening found us sitting on Ms. Kathy's couch having a deeply emotional conversation in a dark room bathed in candle light. We held hands and talked without looking at each other. Ms. Kathy hugged me to comfort me about something and just held me in her arms. Then she kissed my neck. It was a slow deliberate sensual kiss. My body reacted with stiffness on the outside but warm tingles on the inside. I didn't move. I said nothing. The next time I was over to Ms. Kathy's house we sat in the same scenario but this time she kissed my lips. I didn't respond at first but the second time she kissed my lips I kissed her back. We went on for months making out on her couch, kissing and touching with our clothes on. Eventually we moved to touch under our clothes. She touched me and showed me how to touch her. Eventually we were having full-blown sex on some kind of a regular basis.

After some time, the pain seemed to begin and end with her. She brought the pain that I was experiencing at home to the surface and added her own layers onto my pile. I had wet the bed in my sleep as a little girl into my teen years. I couldn't explain why it kept happening or why I slept so hard and couldn't wake up to go to the bathroom. I couldn't tell my mom what I dreamed about or feared. I learned after a few attempts that sharing fears is a weakness. Telling the truth is frowned upon unless it's to benefit the one in charge. I was never in charge. Even when I was in charge of something in the house—like chores or my younger siblings—I didn't feel in charge. I was always nervous that something would go wrong. I didn't want to be in charge when someone got hurt or if the house burned down, because I wasn't great at handling big meals yet, for example.

I wanted freedom from responsibility so badly. I remember writing in my journal and on my computer all the time. I had an old desktop computer that a school program had donated years before. We didn't have any internet or money to update it so I used it just to write short stories and to journal. I saved everything to multiple floppy disks noting that it would be material for my books in the future. I read all the time and dreamed of having different experiences that made me feel free.

Ms. Kathy made me feel free most of the time. I didn't have to take care of anyone but myself when I was with her. It wasn't until much later that I realized she had effectively shifted my responsibilities from my family to her. I did actually end up taking care of her. In fact, I took care of her more than I took care of myself. I did whatever was necessary to make sure she was happy with me. For instance, I helped her do paperwork for her job because she was always behind.

As time went on, I helped her meet professionals and other persons of interest to her. I helped her meet men she wanted to date. I even helped her pay her bills with my scholarship money. Not regular everyday utility bills but big credit-card bills and long-past-due bills with high balances. I had spent thousands of dollars on her before my college saw a penny of my scholarship money. I just wanted to help her. I had no idea that she was taking advantage of me on that level at the time. I truly loved her.

Ms. Kathy had played such a large role in my life for so many years. But at the age of twenty-two, I finally cut her off from my life. I was more than ready for her to leave me alone but battled the feelings of loneliness once she was gone. For years she had tried to keep me away from my friends and family. I didn't realize it at first but after a while I would ask questions about her behavior. I wondered why she always had an attitude if I ever wanted to hang out with some friends or go on a date. Or even if I wanted to go visit a family member during the holidays. I didn't quite understand her reactions because they usually conflicted with her verbal encouragement to experience those very same things.

Around the time that I was brave enough to ask about the inconsistencies in her attitude, she started crying a lot. It seemed as though crying was her escape. She would cry and I would feel bad, and then not do whatever it was that upset her.

Until I didn't. One day I just didn't care. I was tired of her dramatics. I was frustrated with her trying to run my life, and especially disheartened by the rejection that I felt way too often. This space that I moved into caused her to try another approach: sex. She would wriggle out of sex as often as possible with the crying and "not today, we have to stop doing this." But on those days when I couldn't take the frustration anymore or when she would do something blatantly mean and possessive, she would then eagerly initiate sex with me. By the time I caught on, I was wrapped up in the drama of it all. I saw it coming every time and made a decision depending on how I felt that day. I would fight her and call her out on it, or go with it and move on. I'm not even sure how I stuck it out so long.

Lessons learned

These were my first experiences of truly understanding my circumstances. I was susceptible to predators because

I was unaware that I lacked the love and attention that children actually need. I didn't even know how bad my home circumstances were until Kathy assisted me with that awareness from her perspective. What was meant to be selfish and predatory actually turned out to be good for me in these ways.

I could not see clearly; therefore I could not change my circumstances. I didn't even know what to ask for in those days. I realized that people can be predators on another level in that they can show up as heroes—only to get you to do their bidding. She showed me that my lack of awareness was one of the most dangerous things for my future. If I didn't take control of my own narrative by guiding my awareness, anyone could use my trauma for their personal gain.

I realized that I needed to become more self-aware, in a way that really worked for me. As a young adult, just breaking free from an abuser, I was not very trusting at all. Luckily, there was one area where I was more open to feedback than any other. It was in my job. I had started a wonderful career right out of college and wanted to learn all that I could to grow and be great at my job. This was a part of my lesson.

Sometimes it seems like nothing in life is going well. But if we look deliberately, we can see that there is an area that we can use for our good. Since work was the only area of life that I was truly open to, I learned how to set goals and track them. I learned how to work with others and asked myself questions about why people responded the way they did. I asked myself why I thought a certain way about others as I went through my work days. Working in sales was definitely a godsend in my life because it was an opportunity to learn how people think. I learned so much about my wiring, just by doing my job. Then, I learned about Awareness Assistance by becoming that for my customers. I was the person who reminded them about their wiring, what they were blatantly aware of versus what they weren't aware of, and about what they actually believed. I was effectively demonstrating the skills that I needed to change my own life and heal my own trauma.

As the early years of my career moved on, I practiced being the AA for my customers, friends, and family members. I was really good at it in those contexts but still hadn't understood how to apply it to my *own* life in the same way. I believe my saving grace was the effort I put into growing as a person. Reading a variety of books and following successful people's work helped me to see another way.

This is all hindsight of course, but it is a real example of how the brain works to help us find answers. I said to myself at twenty-two years old, "I want to be free from Kathy, take care of myself, and have fun." I didn't know how to do that, since I had been under her thumb from the age of fourteen, and I completely relied on Kathy to take care of me—physically, mentally, emotionally, and more. Because I set it up as a desire, my brain took me on the journey I needed in order to get what I wanted. Growing at work was the beginning of me truly seeing myself.

Taking the first steps

You must practice and improve your self-awareness to transform trauma into power. A good beginning point is to understand why self-awareness is important to you. Everyone can use self-awareness, but when we're living in survival mode, self-awareness isn't high on the to-do list. First I came to understand the importance of awareness. I knew I wanted to be free from my abuser. That desire was strong enough to push me to the next level. But it took years for me to gain that level of strength; and it still came with a high level of distrust, which I had to work around.

Begin by evaluating and understanding your desires; acknowledge your feelings (to yourself and not necessarily to others); practice doing things for yourself; reflect on how far you've come, and how; and understand your emotional triggers.

~Ɔ

- Take a moment to write down your truest desires in your journal. What feelings come up when you consider what you really want? Write them down as well.
- Next, reflect on some progress you've made in one of those areas—no matter how small—and write out an example of your growth.

I believe that being your own assistant in awareness is rooted in understanding your emotional triggers. It is a wonderful thing to have people in your life whom you trust and can turn to for assistance. However, the truth is that people aren't always available or qualified to help you. Another's perspective will not always align with your own truth. Plus, it is very dangerous to your mental/emotional health to rely on others for your personal awareness.

You have the answers for your life. Find them by building trust with yourself, being courageous, asking foundational questions, and meditating. You will better see and understand your results. You are most powerful when you practice and master being your own Awareness Assistant.

Chapter Five

Foundational Knowing

Chuck and Chuck 2.0

In these next chapters, I will start by showing you how I lost my inner knowing and esteem; they go hand in hand. There is a price in experience for every lesson learned. In order for you to truly understand the price paid for the wisdom of the WAAKE Healing Methodology, I must bring you into more past experiences with me.

I am a bit fuzzy on the details of how he and I met but I remember it was a social scene. Maybe at a bar or club that was hosting a party for young business people. He watched me from across the room for a while; then he came through the crowd of people to talk to me. I remember that I found his energy fun, and we connected from there. As we started hanging out I found that *fun* was indeed correct. We had a lot of fun doing all the things I enjoyed doing—like trying new restaurants and bars, taking random small trips, hosting small gatherings where we mixed drinks for our friends and told bullshit stories just to laugh. He was also into things that I was interested in but didn't know the next steps for how to attain—such as riding motorcycles, scuba diving, and building muscle in the gym.

He taught me a lot about things I was interested in that he had already experienced, and piqued my interest about other things, which motivated me to do my own research. I enjoyed all the fun and the learning. But there was something about him that simply didn't sit right with me. At the time, I couldn't see clearly what the problem was but I broke up with him every four to six months for two years. Something eerily familiar would come up and make me feel threatened; but I always seemed to fall short of a real explanation of my feelings. He would do something that felt controlling, or it felt like he was not in control of his temper, or he would try to pressure me into making our relationship more serious than I wanted it to be. And I would run away.

In hindsight, I realize that he was completely controlling and manipulative. He was all of the men I had dated previously rolled into one intelligent, experienced, covert narcissistic snake. In fact, he was my Chuck 2.0—and I was completely blind to that fact at the time.

Chuck was my worst nightmare on constant replay. He was the main reason that I didn't trust and mostly disliked men. Chuck was an active part of my life for about six years, and in that time he did some major emotional and psychological damage. He came into my life as my mother's boyfriend when I was ten years old. The man who I had called Dad had died months before. He died at home, in his bed, while the rest of the family danced around and played cards in celebration of his return home after a brief stay in the county jail. All the kids played in the rooms, periodically bothering the adults at the card table for snacks or a sip of beer. We came out to dance to our favorite blues or stepping songs, then ran off to jump around in our bedrooms. Dad was in the room alone for a long time so I asked about him and my mom said he was tired. She went in to check on him later in the night and screamed loud enough to shake the whole apartment building.

Everybody panicked and scrambled to see what was wrong. The adults pushed the kids back to our rooms and told us to stay there but I had already seen his limp body face down at the foot of the bed. The kids piled in the room and speculated in whispers. I sat quietly with tears in my eyes knowing he was gone but afraid to accept it. After all, Mom had just had my baby brother and there were four of us kids now. Plus, I thought he was a great dad—as far as I knew about dads. My biological father was certified crazy, and this man had been in my life since I was two years old. He was kind, loving, and fun, and he always knew how to make money so that we were never hungry when he was around.

He apparently wasn't a good husband though, since it was through him and my mom fighting that my siblings and I were introduced to domestic violence. They fought hard and often it seems. Dad got into trouble a lot for his hustling and went away sometimes. Those times were hard because Mom would disappear for long hours and even days, and we were often hungry. When Dad was around, sometimes we went without lights, or without toothpaste to brush our teeth, but we had candles and soap, and we always had food. He would take us out with him in the summer time to sell things like toys and balloons with beans in them to make noise. We also sold candy Icee cups out of our house to make money in the summer. Dad made me feel strong and sure of myself, as he convinced me that I was the most mature little girl ever, and capable of taking care of my family. He affectionately called me "little woman."

After Dad died we stayed with friends we called cousins for a while, and although we were sad, everything seemed to be going okay. When we returned home, Mom soon after returned to what she told us was working double shifts as a nurse. But she was really simply "running the streets" as we would say. We went back to not having food, washing clothes in the bathtub with regular soap, and waiting at the window for hours or even *days*, watching for her to walk down the path to our apartment building. Basically, life sucked.

One day she didn't come home alone but brought with her a friend named Chuck. They brought food home and she introduced him to us all, saying he would be around from then on. He seemed nice enough at first but honestly we were mostly interested in the food. We had seen men come and go, so we weren't excited to embrace someone new. He stayed all day that day and even spent the night. It got late and we decided to have a family movie night. We spread out on the couch and living room floor watching movies until we all fell asleep.

The next day as I was bathing my younger sister, she told me how Chuck had touched her the night before as we all slept. He was next to her on the floor and molested her throughout the night. I was furious and scared, and ran to tell my mom what my sister—five years younger than I—had just told me.

Honestly, this was my chance. It was my chance to tell on a predator and feel safe again. I had been molested before, several times, before this guy showed up. But I had never told Mom because I was afraid. The people who touched me or made me do things to them were people I knew and trusted at some point. They were even people I loved and still had to see at family gatherings and such. I simply couldn't work up the nerve to tell the truth about those experiences, especially since I took it to heart when they told me that nobody would believe me. After all, nobody was really paying attention to me anyway beyond making sure I cooked, took care of the younger kids, and cleaned the house.

Now that I had a chance to let it all out about a stranger, it was much easier to tell. My mom came into the bathroom where my sister still sat in the tub and listened to us tell her the story. She asked questions to confirm where and how he touched her, and then left saying she would take care of it. Chuck was still in the house so we heard them arguing in the bedroom. And then we heard him leaving. My siblings and I celebrated, thinking that Mom had put him out to protect us. She had finally chosen us over other priorities, we thought. I talked to my big brother about it all after Chuck left, and he comforted me as usual. We vowed to take care of each other and our younger siblings better, to protect each other from predators like him from now on.

We felt strong and victorious. And most importantly we had our mom back, which is all we ever truly wanted. This lasted for two days…and then Chuck walked back into our home. Dumbfounded, we asked what he was doing there. Mom didn't say much about it except that we were to respect him as an adult. Chuck, on the other hand, had a whole different attitude. He walked in like he owned the place and dared us to look at him too hard. He got in our faces and cursed us out, saying how we'd been running over our mom but now there was a new authority in town who would show us a child's place. We were completely deflated as we looked at our mom with disbelief. Chuck especially seemed to dislike me. I felt that I would never feel safe again. And I never did.

For the next six years of my life, this guy did everything in his power to ruin my life. From my perspective he had a lot of power and I didn't know how to get free of him. At one point I even tried to commit suicide because I was so miserable in that household. I could feel his frustration grow as he talked down to me on a regular basis and put me on punishment for anything. It got to the point where I was away from the house as much as possible, doing things in school and working after school. I would come home at night with dinner for myself since it was usually late, and Chuck would randomly taunt me at the dining room table and knock my food to the floor. He would physically push me around at times and threaten to do whatever he wanted to me. I knew he wanted to rape me but he didn't think he would get away with it. I lived in fear every day but somehow I had the strength to fight back. It seemed my little bit of fight was the only thing keeping me safe from being completely taken.

This guy was physically imposing but more dangerous because he was smart, strategic, and mentally and emotionally abusive. He was ex-military and reminded us of that on a regular basis. He would punish us with things like scrubbing the floor with a toothbrush, and "the pit." He had so much fun with his military torture terms. The pit was basically an extreme quarantine from anything and anyone we loved. He would separate the younger siblings from the older ones on a regular basis, as it was much easier to control them with candy and play time. For us older children, he would separate us in different rooms and make us get in the bed. We weren't allowed to get out of bed except for the bathroom. We weren't allowed any entertainment except for books. Luckily we both enjoyed reading. We also weren't allowed to see or talk to our siblings or to our mom. If they were caught trying to interact with us, he would punish them as well. They quickly learned to follow his rules.

As time went on, Chuck gained a stronghold on the entire household. My older brother and I still fought back in our own way but that landed us tortured and we were eventually kicked out of the house. First, it was my big brother Leon who was kicked out. He was one year older than I was and lasted almost four years before Chuck got him sent to juvenile detention. The crazy thing is that my brother was a very good and responsible kid. He had never done anything illegal or violent—until Chuck just pushed him over the edge. He tried to protect me against the man one night, and got sent away. They took him away in the middle of the night and didn't tell the rest of us where he was or what had happened to him. I had to beg counselors at school to do some research to find my brother. Until then, he had been my best friend and the only stability in that household. Oh yes, Chuck was very smart to separate the two of us. Without my brother Leon I was weaker and more vulnerable than I had ever been.

My younger siblings were a lost cause at that point. They were completely under Chuck's spell. I couldn't confide in them without them telling him everything. They also didn't tell me anything but hid from me and treated me like I was the enemy. Of course, this was all taught to them over time. Chuck would do this interesting thing that played a trick on your mind. Not regular mind games but ones that made you feel crazy, and you would truly think you might be crazy for feeling abused.

It was kind of like when a man rapes a woman and then says it's her fault for wearing a short skirt to the bar; but then he takes it a bit further, and gathers a jury of other people who are also rapists—unbeknownst to her—and asks them to confirm that her rape was indeed her fault. They confirm with compassion in their voice and sincerity in their eyes, and she is utterly confused. Someone in the jury is a person she knows and trusts, and this person actually questions if the rape even really happened. "You seem confused," he says. She knows it happened and it was wrong but nobody seems to understand or believe her side of the story.

Now the woman questions herself, and her once very clear memory of the rape details are blurry. She doesn't know what to believe in her own mind or if she can even trust herself. Chuck would play this game with me on a regular basis. Whatever I complained about was counteracted by a jury of my younger siblings, with my mom as the judge. Since I couldn't see past my mother's flaws, I continued to trust her, even while knowing that it was wrong. My internal compass was very sharp and I knew what they were doing; but somehow I still couldn't control my mind or reaction to it. I didn't know about the subconscious mind at the time so had no idea how mind control really works. I had the feeling of knowing, but felt utterly powerless to stop the manipulation.

I took the hits and stood strong against them, not realizing the emotional, mental, and spiritual damage it was doing on the inside. I built up endurance and came back every day willing to openly love and give to my mom and siblings. Ironically, loving them just felt easier.

Our knowing and our identity

Remember, the *K* in the WAAKE Healing Methodology references Knowing.

- Where does your knowing lie?
- What are your foundational beliefs?

We all create our personalities based on the various experiences we had growing up. Our beliefs are created in the same way. The difference is that one can fake a different personality for a while—but a deeply seated belief shows itself as more of a reflex.

Much of my relationship ideals for better or worse were forged in those pivotal years with my mom and Chuck. As painful a reality as it is, I was wired to be codependent and susceptible to narcissistic personalities; thus, my belief system was grounded in a lack of self-love, independence, or boundaries. I was wired to give until it hurts while ignoring my own needs. I was wired to be nice instead of truthful. The painful experiences I endured in my life were at the root because of my subconscious wiring and foundational knowing.

We have covered wiring in previous chapters but now I want you to see clearly that wiring is directly related to knowing. It is one thing to understand how you were wired as a child and another thing to see how that wiring contributes to your foundational knowing. I had to get my foundation stable in my own knowing for any hope of healing past trauma.

Our foundational knowing creates our identity. A person's identity is the hardest thing to change because it is the thing humans cling to the most. Knowing "who you are" is essential to survival. Human beings are wired to survive first. So to change our identity might feel threatening to our survival. It really isn't threatening in today's world but our beautiful brains are wired for survival so it will do everything in its power to keep us safe. For a person who has experienced trauma this means the brain will remember all of that trauma and tell you over and over again how to avoid it. You will live in survival mode forever on this track.

Changing your foundational story

So, how do you change tracks? You change your foundational story.

Your main pivotal story, which created your wiring and knowing, might still be what happened; but *you have the power to change the meaning of why those things happened*—which can then switch off the trauma response in the brain. This is only half the story of my realization of my own foundational knowing. I didn't get to the solutions until I realized how it had affected my self-esteem. These were the experiences that took me to my "rock bottom," where I was finally ready and able to do whatever it took to get up and truly heal. Keep reading to see how my life experiences connected to show me how I was living out my foundational knowing.

Chapter Six

Roots in Your Story

Telling the truth

I can still remember clearly the life event that allowed my Chuck 2.0 to really get me in his grip. I went on a trip to Las Vegas with my mom and sister, and had one of the worst experiences of my life. I'm not sure how we got on the subject but somehow we came to the worst subject possible: Chuck. We strolled through the casino looking around and talking. They were running low on money so I bought us lunch. Mom asked for money to gamble and I gave a polite *no* to her request. Since I had chips left, they went on about which games I should play and how to play to hit big. I tried a few of them with low enthusiasm and lost some money. Then I stopped, saying I would save the rest for something I was comfortable with: the blackjack table at another hotel. My sister made a comment alluding to me being cheap, and I replied with a snappy comment about her using her own money to gamble, which she didn't have. The fight began.

She spewed nasty remarks at me in a now-elevated tone, accusing me of being selfish and never being around for the family. My irritation grew quickly as I listened to her disregard all of my efforts to be close with my mom and siblings. I replied with a voice that was calm but laced with heat.

"Do you mean all the times I would drive over to your house to visit or try to pick you up and take you out somewhere? Or all the times I would come by just to give y'all money for food, bus passes, or school clothes? When you weren't even going to school. You took hundreds of my dollars saying you needed it for school, yet ditched school every day. I tried to talk to y'all—to connect—but all you did was lie to me about everything. Or say nothing at all. Yet, you had no problem showing up with a phone call when you wanted some money. How do you think that makes me feel? When the people I took care of—fed, bathed, took to and from school, helped with homework, and protected—now treat me like a stranger—"

"You didn't protect us," she interrupted. "You left us! All you think about is yourself. Everything got worse when you left. We got evicted and you were nowhere to be found. You were out living a good life with Ms. Kathy."

"Interesting that you would blame *me* for all of that when your mother was right there with you," I said through clenched teeth. "I was a kid, too; I wasn't supposed to be taking care of y'all. I did it because if I didn't it wouldn't happen at all. I did it because I love y'all. But you're blaming me for adult problems that you should be blaming your mother for. First of all, I didn't leave, *she put me out.* Then when I tried to call and see y'all just days later she cursed me and my cousin out and told us we would never see y'all again. That was her plan and her remedy for whatever she thought I had done wrong."

My mom jumped in the conversation to defend herself. "I never put you out. You asked to leave and I let you leave."

My heart was pounding hard as I tried to keep my cool. "*Bullshit*! I asked to leave two weeks before you put me out. I asked to move in with my cousin and you said *no*. Then two weeks later, I came home to all of my stuff in boxes and thrown in the dumpster behind the house. Then you literally dragged me out of the house and beat me for two blocks until you took my money and sent me away. Is that how you 'let' people leave?"

We went back and forth for an hour—with my mom and sister defending my mother's actions and decisions. They verbally jumped on me like I was the one factor that had made their life go awry. I couldn't believe it. I was completely taken aback by their words, by their thoughts and beliefs about how life should work.

My sister told me I wasn't supposed to have gone to college but should have stayed back to take care of them.

My mom mostly let my sister attack me for her, unless I said something that painted her in a bad light or something that might influence my sister to think differently.

I was heartbroken. Had they brought me all the way to Vegas just waiting on the opportunity to make me feel like shit? I didn't feel like shit because of what they said. Of course, none of that resonated as truth with me. But I felt like shit because the people I loved so deeply, people I couldn't let go of, had made me out to be the cause of all of their problems—and more deeply than I had ever realized. They laid it on thick, attack after filthy attack, until I simply cried and walked away.

They weren't letting me get away that easily. Now they felt they had the upper hand. They felt strong in their conviction that I was a bad person, sister, and daughter. So they followed me, spewing their lies and accusations. I knew there was nothing that I could say to change their minds or make them think clearly. I did my best to stand my ground, knowing that there was something wrong with their view of the world.

But that didn't stop the pain. The pain was excruciating. My ears rang and my head spun around in large dramatic circles. My heart literally hurt in my chest as I listened to how they felt about me. I realized that my search for them—my efforts to reconnect and to have the family love that I so desired—were futile.

I whirled around to spew my own mean truths. "I'm so happy I left. If I didn't I would've ended up as confused and miserable as y'all. Mom, you've got her out here as your trained attack dog, when *you're* the one who continuously put us in harm's way. You brought that child molester into our lives and did nothing about the abuse. You were too busy running the streets instead of going to work. *That's* why you got evicted! How the hell do you have two working adults plus me—who gave you money all the time? Well, when you weren't stealing it from my after-school job. And you get Section 8 and food stamps, and still get evic—"

She grabbed my face to shut me up.

It took everything in me not to hit her with my fist. I jerked away. "Don't touch me. You haven't earned the right." I walked away to the bathroom. This time they didn't follow me but lingered around the entrance. They were so mad that I wondered if I should fear being physically attacked. I wouldn't put it past them. I came out of the stall to find my mom standing near the sink area. The bathroom was fairly empty with one woman washing her hands and us. I ignored her as I walked to the sink to wash my hands.

She took a deep breath. "Y'all are sisters. You need to be better than this. It's important that you stick together."

I ignored her.

She showed some sign of an emotion other than anger for the first time and continued, "I know I could've done better. I know I wasn't always the best mother and left you to do a lot. That was a lot on your shoulders and I'm really sorry for that. You didn't feel safe around Chuck and I get it. I did the best that I could."

I looked at her through the mirror with tears in my eyes. "Oh, you did your best, huh?! Does that include all the lies you told my siblings to get them to hate me? Does that include taking advantage of me every chance you get? Even now! You're saying all this stuff to me but you made sure it's just you and me. Why wouldn't you say it in front of my sister since it's so important for us to love each other and stick together?"

A security guard walked in the bathroom asking if everything was okay.

We replied with a dry *yes*.

She asked us to leave the bathroom and that area of the casino floor. People had witnessed us walking through the casino during our intense yelling match, and that, I'm sure, was bad for business.

We left the bathroom and walked our separate ways. I didn't know where I was going but I had to think of how to get away from them. Our flight was leaving the next day but I didn't even want to be around them one more night.

I walked and walked. . .until I ran into my sister sitting outside of a Cinnabon. I felt so bad for her. I could see how she had gotten to where she was in her mind. I could see the intense training that she'd endured, fueled with hunger, homelessness, and a sudden shift in responsibility after I was gone. I sat next to her quietly.

She let the tears fall and spoke softly. "He kept doing it. All those years he would touch me and do stuff to me. Then it got to the point where he would rape me. He raped me all the time for years after you left."

My heart dropped into my stomach. My tears rolled hot down my face. "I'm so sorry. I didn't know." I cried harder. "Why didn't you tell me when I was still there? Why didn't you tell Mom?"

"She was there," she snapped. "She was right in the other room when he would come in my room and get on top of me. What was I supposed to say?"

I was furious. My emotions of pain, anger, and sorrow made me feel sick to my stomach. We sat there for what felt like hours. . .quiet. . .crying on and off. Finally, we walked outside and around the corner to the entrance to our hotel.

There we found Mom standing outside smoking a cigarette. I walked past her and went inside the building, leaving my sister outside at my mom's side.

The rest of the night was a blur. That's how it was, wasn't it? It didn't matter that they had their own truths when alone. The game is that you find a partner with a common enemy and stick together. I was the common enemy. My mom knew she was wrong on many fronts, and my sister knew as well, but somehow she couldn't see enough to say the truth to our mother. She whispered truth in secret, knowing that nobody would ever believe she'd said those things to me. They stuck together—and that gave them strength and power to come against people like me.

I was a fool for trying to make the blind woman see.

I don't think I slept that night but the next morning I found myself in the airport with my mom and sister, staring at the delayed notice on the board. The weather in Chicago was unpredictable as usual. Most flights came and went with no problem but sometimes a huge storm could brew right in the middle of one's travel and cause delays or even cancellations. I guess that was my life in a nutshell at this point.

We waited around for hours until they finally told us the flight was canceled due to a Chicago snowstorm. Though not surprised, I was devastated. *Now what?!*

I began a hotel search on my phone while my mom and sister talked amongst themselves. I was ready to leave them behind and try to enjoy the extra day in Vegas alone. But I also struggled with the idea of leaving them behind. I knew they didn't have any money and would be stuck sleeping in the airport for a day or two. I found a hotel and waited quietly for them to approach me with a sob story.

This couldn't be happening to me. After all I had gone through with them just the day before. *And now I have to take care of them?* I prayed silently and asked God to give me the right thing to do. None of my ideas felt right in that moment. Everything felt extremely uncomfortable and inconvenient for me.

I heard them on the phone calling friends, asking for money. After a while they came back to me saying they needed help because nobody had money to loan them for a hotel stay. I started to lecture them about being that broke that they didn't even have an emergency fund. Who goes on vacation without emergency money? But I just sat there quietly fuming. I felt like I had to help them. They were still my mom and sister, after all. That feeling made me simultaneously mad and sad. How would I ever be free from them if they could do and say whatever they wanted against me and I would still take care of them? *What kind of wimp am I?*

In that moment I decided that I had to cut them off. "After we get out of Vegas it is over. I quit."

I told them they could stay with me in my hotel but they needed to find money for food. They gave a dull thanks and continued to call people.

We arrived at the new hotel minutes later as it was close to the airport. It was a nice, large, all-suite hotel that made me feel more comfortable than the last. I picked a non-smoking suite and informed them that they couldn't smoke in the room. Unfortunately, everything I had with me already stank of cigarette smoke. I hated the smell of cigarette smoke but had tried to deal with it until this point. I checked us into our comfortable suite which had enough space for the three of us to sleep in separate beds. I bought dinner for everyone, and died a bit inside with every dollar I spent or shared with them. We mostly existed together in silence. Once settled I broke away and wandered the casino floor playing games and drinking.

I couldn't wrap my mind around what was happening. After calling the airline multiple times, the earliest flight we could get out of town was Wednesday morning. That was two extra nights with these people who hated me, who caused me pain with every glance. I sulked and drank rum, walking around with my thoughts. *How can I be free from these feelings, from this pain?*

That night went by quickly. The next day I found myself up doing the same thing. I ate, drank, and drank some more while walking around with my thoughts. Eventually my mom and sister caught up with me on the casino floor. They were gambling. I guess someone had sent them money. I was thankful for that since I was avoiding them and didn't even want to buy them a meal on this day.

My sister made smart remarks under her breath as my mom tried to make small talk with me. I halfway replied and suggested they get their own room since my sister had so many issues with me. Mom instructed my sister to stop and she moved away from us. I was disgusted that I was spending money on these monsters. *As soon as they get a little money they don't try to pay me back but gamble it away instead.*

I walked away, leaving my mom at the table to gamble alone. She found me later and asked to sit down to talk. I reluctantly sat at an empty table and waited for her to speak.

She made some uncomfortable movements to get adjusted before speaking. Finally, she asked about my current boyfriend Josh. She wanted to know what was up with our relationship. I didn't say much about it as I really didn't feel like talking about boys with her. What did she know about relationships? I mentioned that he had asked me to move in with him but I hadn't made up my mind. Mom went on to tell me how Josh reminded her of Chuck. She made that comment and looked at me silently.

I wondered if she could see the anger in my face or the steam coming out of my ears. *After everything she's put me through, how does she expect me to feel about such a comment*? I asked, "In what way?"

She didn't have any specifics. She said he just reminded her of her deranged rapist of an ex-boyfriend.

I replied in a controlled tone of voice, "So you don't know *how* or *why* he reminds you of Chuck but that's what you want to leave me with? You've told me that everything about me is wrong and selfish and not up to your standards. And then you turn around and. . .what? Tell me I'm just like you? I chose the same dude that you did to ruin your life and your children's lives?" I stood up. "He is nothing like Chuck. Fuck you." With that generously spewed hate and righteous indignation, I walked away.

I was confused, though. *Why would she say that to me*? Especially after all the other things she's said to me on this trip. Was that her last attempt to stomp on my heart? Maybe I seemed too controlled in my emotions so she felt the need to stab me good one last time. I don't know for sure but I do know that now I felt even more resolved in my decision to cut them off.

I would move on with my life without my mother and younger siblings, and I would be happy. I had to do it. This had to work, or I would simply perish from feelings of worthlessness and deep depression.

Rationalizing

Upon returning home, I avoided people until I could pull myself together. My boyfriend had asked me to move in with him before I left and my immediate reaction was to decline. I couldn't verbalize why. I now felt that I should make it work—that we could make our relationship work. I kept thinking back to "the 80/20 rule" that people often spoke of. If I could only have eighty percent of what I want or need anyway, was this lack of twenty percent in him that serious? I rationalized the difficulty of the relationship and even wrote out a list. The positive column was much longer than the negative column as I finished the list. In hindsight, I should have *weighed* each item as well. Then I would've found that the negative column far outweighed the positive column in importance to my future and my happiness.

I went with what I had, and finally saw Josh in person. We talked over dinner about the horrible experience I'd had on the trip. He listened carefully, periodically inserting a strong opinion about why they did something or how wrong they were. He compared my relationship with my mom with his relationship with his mother. He talked about how he had cut her off for similar reasons and also because she didn't support him. I let him go on about his feelings and comparisons until he was done. I was exhausted just talking about the whole ordeal so it felt good that he understood me to that extent.

By the end of the night, Josh declared that I didn't need my family because *he* was my new family. There was a weird gleam in his eye with this declaration. I remember noticing this gleam or spark every so often. It was so unnatural. I was naturally a romantic, and mostly verbally open about my feelings. My love was written on my face, as they say. He tried to write his love on his face sometimes—and it always came out a bit odd. It felt like he was deliberately showing me he cared through his forced facial expressions instead of it just flowing naturally.

I didn't know what to think about the feeling I got from this. I had told him there wasn't enough of an emotional connection and that I needed to feel more connected to him. Maybe this was his way of being more connected. *I shouldn't punish him for that; right?*

I shook off all my doubt and took his words to heart. I would keep moving forward without them and start my own family here with him. A few days later he asked if I had made a decision about moving in with him, and I agreed to do so. This process was tough for me as I really didn't like his house. I loved my own house and the coziness of it. His house felt cold and dusty, like a bachelor pad. Not a place to build a family. But I moved in anyway.

Change your story

You have already read a bit of how that worked out for me. My mom was right—in that Josh was a narcissist, like Chuck was. I was heading down my darkest path yet—and I had no idea it was happening.

With such strong foundational knowing experiences, how could I heal and move forward? I wasn't sure if that were really possible. I thought that I would suffer deep depression my entire life. So, what made the difference in my healing?

Changing my story made the difference.

When I bring this up—changing your story—people often get irritated and remind me of how true their own story is. This was my initial blockage, too. I couldn't see past the truth of everything that had happened in my life. It surely happened, and it made me the person I had become. I had been a victim of my circumstances, and actually I was a miracle because I'd "made it out." I survived.

I was deeply traumatized and wounded even though I was free from that environment. It *looked like* I had made it out—but I was so traumatized that I regularly acted in response to trauma—instead of in response to the current moment.

Your story and the meaning you give to it is incredibly important.

Listen to your intuition

As a child, I remember feeling so sure of my decisions. I was in tune with my intuition. My self-esteem was rooted in my self-confidence. Because I kept getting the same unwanted results and life experiences, in my late twenties I finally started to question what I thought was my intuition. Is this intuition from a Higher Power. . .my inner being. . .from God? Or is this learned behavior from my past pain—protection from my amazing brain, which is made to protect me, and won't let me repeat what's painful?

I had to learn how my intuition really sounded and felt. That would require quiet time with myself. I was no stranger to spending time alone. But it was often filled with distractions so that I didn't have to deal with the noise and the pain that my mind and body relived each day.

One day, I decided to try it anyway. I actually sat with my thoughts, as uncomfortable as they were. I asked myself about each thought—if it was something I really believed, or believed only because someone else said I should. I felt an answer in my gut right away. I was shocked at the feeling of certainty. I had experienced certainty before and could point to examples in my life when I was completely certain. I would ace an exam or win over a customer at work or even solve a friend's problem. I knew the feeling—but it was only then that I realized it hadn't been the feeling of certainty all along that I'd used to justify my decisions. It was something else altogether. So I asked more questions of myself.

I received so many answers so quickly, it was like they were just waiting on me to finally ask. Maybe they were sitting there in my brain and body in plain sight—waiting on me to notice them. Either way, I quickly realized how truly unsure I had been of myself for so long.

Being unsure of myself, I looked for answers in religion, counseling, and other people via relationships. I spent years in church, giving all that I had to serving others and the church. I was faithful in tithing and attendance and being a hands-on helper with whatever was needed. I prayed and fasted and danced and preached. I became a lay leader, even an ordained prophetess, and I started ministry school. I just knew that this path would help heal the gaping hole in my heart.

I wanted that to be true so badly. But it never was. I didn't find the relief I searched for. I didn't even feel true love in the church. I did learn a lot and found some answers but they were misinterpreted at the time so I was unable to use the answers in a way that benefited my life. The amount of guilt and self-blame I showered down on myself was poisonous.

The Journey within

I searched and searched for peace. I acted like a chameleon in order to understand different people and how they think and make decisions. This made me successful in my work life but not as successful as I wanted to be—since I was still mainly unfulfilled and often unhappy. Though it was my primary desire, I found no lasting success in my personal relationships. Wanting something so badly that was always just outside of my grasp was frustrating to say the least. First, I blamed others—which was easy since nobody is perfect; and I felt fairly mature in comparison to my peer group.

After some time I thought I needed to take a different approach so I started looking more closely at myself and at how I could be better to get what I wanted. Notice I said I wanted to be better *to get what I wanted*—not just to be fulfilled and happy. At the time I didn't understand the notion of fulfillment, nor did I know what true happiness felt like.

I spent much of my time learning about the art of listening, emotional intelligence, cultural intelligence differences, managing up, and organizational development. I applied maybe half of what I learned, and became very successful in showing others how awesome and worthy they are. My studies and my greater understanding of people gave me a sense of satisfaction and confidence. But I still didn't have lasting personal relationships. Eventually, I started to put myself first but had no idea how to truly do that. My learned behavior, which was rooted in deep trauma, kept taking over my will.

Just to give you an idea of what this was like for me, let's take a look at an example. I can easily recall an experience with my first fiancé. We were having a disagreement about something silly in my opinion but something important in his opinion. I was at the stove cooking dinner when he raised his voice and walked towards me. I panicked. My immediate response was to feel endangered. I truly thought I was in danger—that he was going to harm me physically. This guy was generally a sweet and loving person who had never shown any aggression to me before. But I had seen or experienced something like what he did that night before. The last time it happened, I ended up fighting to protect my dignity and my body.

In effect, I had Post-Traumatic Stress Disorder (PTSD). This knowledge, of course, is hindsight—as I thought my reaction was natural at the time. Looking back, I can see that he was probably just having a passionate moment, trying to get his point across. I can see now that he did not have any true intention to harm me.

As I sat with myself over a period of a few years, asking and answering questions, I slowly uncovered similar examples of me responding to triggers instead of to the true moment. I was finally peeling back the layers. I also noticed how nice and agreeable I was in relationships—almost too nice. The only things that saved me from being a doormat were my fierce need for justice, and me mostly not allowing people to get very close. I seemed to be most susceptible to oppression from the people I allowed into my heart, so I kept it very limited.

Since trauma lives in your mind, body, and genes, it is imperative to see it for what it is and learn your triggers. The ability to break your survival mode habits, and to heal—or at least to manage—your PTSD and your depression is rooted in this understanding of the importance of changing your story.

Visualization

When you change your story, you can be the one to stop perpetuating your own history, and your ancestral trauma history as well. An effective way to change your story can be to literally practice a new story in place of the old one in your mind. When living with PTSD or past trauma, the old stories come up in response to triggers—everyday life events—and cause the individual to relive that experience. Changing the story requires practicing a new story to replace the old one.

Instead of the story that said I would live in depression from losing my family for the rest of my life, I began to imagine me feeling good and settled—whether they were in my life or not. I took time to relax while breathing deeply and I would picture my future self in my mind, feeling good and happy. Sometimes in my mind's eye it was Mother's Day or some other holiday where family would visit and connect. I was careful to envision myself as happy whether there were people around or not. This took some deliberate work. As I created the new story, my mind would often bring up old emotions of sadness or loneliness, if there were no family members around my Thanksgiving table, for example. I would pause, and rewrite that part of the story to condition myself to feel happy.

Sometimes the pain was so deeply wired that I couldn't force a change of state even in my mind. In these instances, it is a good idea to use friends and loved ones to validate your new story. I would sometimes visualize my best friend in my new story telling me how well I had done at overcoming something. Or, how she never thought I'd be able to forgive that person who had hurt me so deeply.

Over time, I got better at the practice of visualization. I got better at controlling my thoughts, asking myself questions and creating new stories for myself. Changing my story changed my life.

I hope this helps you understand how important your story is. There are a few methods of changing your story. My favorite is the practice of retracing a scenario—as New Thought authors like Neville Goddard teach. Retracing is similar to visualization but requires a consistent daily practice so that you can create momentum in how life responds to you. There is an exercise (starting on p. 103) that will walk you through the specifics of retracing in the next chapter.

Sometimes trauma makes it difficult to concentrate on one thing or to sit quietly so that you are able to recreate an experience. The WAAKE Healing Methodology will help you to calm those anxious trauma patterns and begin to change your story. Keep journaling. Give the visualization technique a try and record your thoughts and feelings.

~◡

- Was it difficult to visualize things going differently for you?
- Could you feel the emotions of your new story as strongly as those from your old story?

Read further to understand how to change your story even when you've been severely mentally and emotionally abused.

Chapter Seven

Let's Talk About Narcissism

Narcissistic Personality Disorder (NPD) is defined by the dictionary as a mental condition in which people have an inflated sense of their own importance, a deep need for excessive attention and admiration, troubled relationships, and a lack of empathy for others.

I didn't know anything about narcissism or narcissistic abuse before experiencing this in a relationship—and seeking therapy as a result. It was through months of therapy sessions that I realized that Josh (my daughter's father) and Chuck are narcissists. I'm sure there are other people in my life who are also narcissists, as I was the typical empathetic, overly kind, acceptable person who was in need of love—the type of person that narcissists usually target.

That was the underlying issue. On the surface, I seemed to have it all together. Narcissists only go for people they deem happy and healthy because they need to feed off of these individuals in order to feel relevant. Beyond my underlying vices, I was generally very happy, beautiful, fit, and financially stable. This was the person Josh targeted and tried to take down.

There are some official criteria for NPD that are often not discussed and can be very difficult to spot if you have no personal experience with NPD or are not a qualified expert. I never discount the value of experience—if it has been recognized, if wounds have been treated and healed, or they're in the process of active healing with lessons learned. This means that an experience is well worth the time and effort because *the lessons turn into wisdom.* This wisdom can now be a beaming light in a dark tunnel when the next obstacle or test comes along. Just as important, that beaming light is enough for the individual and countless others who need or desire a path to freedom. One can study a subject for countless hours in school and still never achieve the understanding of the person who experiences that subject first hand.

Here are some official criteria for NPD from the American Psychiatric Association:

- grandiose sense of self-importance
- preoccupation with fantasies of unlimited success, power, brilliance, beauty, or ideal love
- belief they're special and unique and can only be understood by, or should associate with, other special or higher-status people or institutions
- need for excessive admiration
- sense of entitlement
- interpersonally exploitive behavior
- lack of empathy

- envy of others, or a belief that others are envious of them
- demonstration of arrogant and haughty behaviors or attitudes

There are two main types of narcissists, which can make them even trickier to spot if you don't have experience. There is the *covert narcissist* and the *overt narcissist.*

The overt narcissist is rather obvious. You might spend a little time with this person and see the abusive signs, and basically consider this individual to be an asshole in general.

The covert narcissist is much more calculated than the overt narcissist. These individuals use charm and wit to get people to like or favor them. They hide everything real about themselves until they can see a clear path to having the upper hand on their prey. Yes, I said *prey.* They are predators. And generally very good ones.

Josh, my ex, had shown all the signs of being a covert narcissist. People still to this day, years later, ask what happened and make comments about how he seemed so nice and normal when we were dating. After that relationship ended, I would often think about his military background and Chuck's military background. I couldn't help but wonder how much of that learned mental manipulation really helped them become better predators as narcissists.

In general, I had no problem with military people. I had a lot of family in the military so I was accustomed to some of their ideals and general ways of being. In my family this was a positive thing. Dealing with Josh opened my eyes to the possibilities of the other side. The stories I heard from others about their family member changing after war—and their experiences with PTSD—came to life in a different way. Now, I am not blaming the military for their actions or for causing a personality disorder. In the case of Josh and Chuck, it was probably their abusive or neglectful mothers who turned them into narcissists, since both men seemed fascinated primarily with destroying women. I do, however, feel like they have an edge up in mental warfare over the average person who hasn't been trained to be mentally tough or strategic.

This is especially noticeable in romantic relationships. Most men and women are essentially trained to play games in relationships to get what they want. You can see the gender divide in society displayed in assumed gender roles pushed by schools and religion. We also get a clear idea of how these roles play out on TV shows and in movies. Pivotal American TV series like *I Love Lucy* and *Friends* show the world how complicated relationships generally are. We may lie and cheat and hide things, all in an attempt to have the upper hand—to get our needs met and to win the girl or the guy. It can be funny or sad or fascinating to watch such stories as entertainment; but ultimately playing these types of games in real-life relationships creates lots of pain and confusion.

In most cases, what one person thinks is the upper hand is really just a relationship-eroding game, where everyone loses. In the case of the narcissist, there is a real winner. A narcissist plays for keeps and until the bitter end. Since narcissists *aren't capable* of empathy—or even of *somewhat* understanding someone else's needs—they are never as impacted by a relationship's demise as the average person would be. They feel good about tearing things down, about tearing people down. They get mad when they can't hurt the other person enough to feel better about themselves. A relationship with a narcissist goes simply by a different dynamic—which the average person walks into blindly.

The narcissist always has a plan unbeknownst to their companion. People usually don't even notice the signs that they are dating a narcissist until it's too late. Here are some signs that you're dating a narcissist:

- They're charming. . .at first. This is also called "love bombing."
- They hog the conversation, talking about how great they are. They need to gain admiration and often embellish or exaggerate their stories.
- They feed off of your compliments. They seem super-confident but actually they lack self-esteem. They feed off of people who are highly empathic to supply their sense of worth and make them feel powerful. Their super-low self-esteem means that their ego can be bruised easily, which increases their need for compliments.
- They lack empathy. Narcissists don't grasp the concept of feelings, so they are unable to make you feel understood, accepted, or seen.
- They don't have any (or very few) long-term friends. As a result, they might lash out when you want to hang out with your friends.

- They pick at you constantly. It may seem like playful teasing at first but it becomes consistent, bigger, and includes every area of who you are. No area is off limits.

- They gaslight you. Gaslighting is manipulation and emotional abuse—a key trait of narcissism. Some signs of gaslighting include the narcissist telling blatant lies, falsely accusing others, spinning the truth, and continuing these mental/emotional abuse tactics—until ultimately, they can distort your reality. Your reality might be distorted if you:

  ➤ no longer feel like the person you used to be
  ➤ you feel more anxious and less confident than you used to be
  ➤ you often wonder if you're being too sensitive
  ➤ you feel like everything you do is wrong
  ➤ you always think it's your fault when things go wrong
  ➤ you have a sense that something's wrong but you can't identify what it is
  ➤ you often wonder if your responses to your partner are appropriate
  ➤ you make excuses for your partner's behavior

- They dance around defining the relationship.

- They think they're right about everything and never apologize. There is never any true debating or compromise.

- When you show them you're really done, they lash out. They will make it their goal to hurt you for "abandoning" them. Their ego is severely bruised, causing them to feel rage and hate for anyone whom they deem has hurt them—because, of course, everything is the other person's fault.

Going forward

I experienced all of these nasty traits first-hand over several years. It took a long time for me to realize that something *was* actually wrong, and even longer to realize *what* was wrong. Now, after years and layers of healing work, I am light-years ahead of the person I used to be. Now my pain has become wisdom. Now I can help shine a light for others struggling in that dark space.

As a healer and teacher, I don't usually recommend that people dwell on the past. In fact, most times it is beneficial to focus only on the future and on what we want going forward. In my dealings with people, I notice that many have extreme difficulty in letting go because they want so badly to understand the past. This of course was my journey, so it is no surprise that I often run into people who are similar. I had the hardest time moving forward because I held so tightly to the idea that I needed to understand what had happened. That wasn't true. I didn't really need to understand the details and reasons why behind every little experience. I only know that now that I am on the other side of it.

Back then, in my stuck space, going over the past in an effort to understand my missteps turned out to be very helpful. I didn't do it in anger or angst but as a part of my many healing modalities. I learned to meditate and tap into my subconscious mind. As I learned more and more about my subconscious beliefs, I began to ask questions of myself. I talked to myself day and night in an effort to understand who I was and who I was becoming. I talked and talked and journaled until I learned to listen. It was then that things started to clear up. The steps that had led me to where I was were clear. My pain was easing every day because the reasons behind it were more obvious—and usually false. I was more connected to my true self than I had been since childhood.

This story of what happened is an example of my clarity now. I can see how I got lost, and therefore I can easily spot stumbling blocks moving forward.

Can you see all the traits of narcissism in my story? Can you see where you might be dealing with narcissists in your own story?

Some people claim that seeing is believing. This is simply not true. I reached the point where I could finally see what was happening in my life and what had happened in the past to bring me to the current moment. But *seeing wasn't enough* for me to truly change my core beliefs. To truly believe, it took another set of experiences—and time, and lots of hard work.

I had to learn that it is okay to see and not believe, to hear and not quite understand, or to be educated and not really learn. I allowed these experiences to teach me these and other tough life lessons. Each one worked as a steppingstone to get me to the next level. Not knowing is okay—as long as you don't get stuck there. This is true as well for pain and confusion. The lesson is in harnessing the fire and using it *as a tool*—not getting burned beyond repair or dying from the smoke.

How do you change your story?

Our subconscious mind is the creator and director of our conscious life. Often, people make decisions and have specific desires based on their foundational beliefs—beliefs which live in the subconscious mind. Our subconscious mind has a story running on a loop that tells us who we are. Luckily, we have the power to change our subconscious mind so that we can enable it to play the story the way we prefer.

The first step in altering your subconscious is to get quiet in meditation. Meditation allows you to pause the momentum of all those negative thoughts and wiring so that you can begin to turn them around. It is really hard to force positivity on yourself or anyone on a conscious level while the subconscious is still running on old wiring.

Once you have learned to stop thought and slow the momentum of negative thoughts and ideals, then you can began replacing them with the thoughts and ideas that you want to manifest in your life. The key is to do this input with the appropriate emotions. Many people preach affirmations to change your life. Affirmations can be helpful to make you feel better for a period of time but affirmations by themselves rarely allow a person to create lasting change in their circumstances.

Retracing Exercise

Try this:

Every night before you drift off to sleep, trace your entire day in your mind the way it was but change certain things that you wish were different. Make this a practice. Every night, think of your day as if it were completely ideal—and feel the emotions of that great day in your body. This is how it feels when your wishes have been fulfilled by your own subconscious mind. As you get proficient at this practice, you can use the same method in meditation and in your daily waking life to create your ideal day, career, relationship, happiness, and whatever else you want to express.

Even if you have endured severe abuse, it is helpful to practice this strategy of rewriting your day. The idea is to start at an easy place that is rooted in the current moment as much as possible. In time, you will grow stronger and then be able to look back on past experiences that hold you in their grip, and rewrite the entire experience to make it ideal—or at least less painful.

These methods require practice. If you are consistent, it will become easier over time and you will begin to see the weight of trauma lift off your shoulders.

Change the meaning of your story

It is important to rewrite your trauma stories to match your ideal experience. However, if you only retrace memories in an effort to rewrite experiences, you will find the journey long and hard, and your progress will be short-lived. It is just as important to change the *meaning* that you have assigned to your story. We give meaning to everything in our lives. Sometimes we rely on the ideals set by collective society to govern our own story's meaning, and other times we create our individual meaning based on specific experiences.

Trauma will usually yield a disempowering meaning to our life's circumstances.

Imagine taking that traumatic experience and, being the powerful being that you are, making a solid decision that it *did not* make you a victim. Maybe you decide that the trauma doesn't define you. You could decide that it was actually an experience that seemed horrible on the surface yet it served to fuel your expansion. Now you know more clearly what you want in life, who you are, and how you can contribute to the world in your unique way.

The new meaning of that traumatic story is one consistent decision away. And it will set you free.

Breaking your trauma history

As I healed, I stumbled upon many books, teachers, spiritual healers and research, which helped me to understand my plight. The first book that reached me in a new way is *It Didn't Start With You: How Inherited Family Trauma Shapes Who We Are and How to End the Cycle* by Mark Wolynn. I had read and heard lectures about perpetuating family trauma but didn't fully understand the implications. After my last narcissistic relationship, I was desperate to understand my journey, and this book helped me to put things into perspective.

Wolynn talks about how individuals inherit family trauma in their genes, which keeps them stuck or bound in different ways, making their life's journey more difficult. Once I understood how trauma actually shows up in our genes, I was able to look at my family and see the trickle-down effect of serious trauma. In my family, there is no way to know exactly where the trauma started. In fact, it is likely that the trauma dates all the way back to African slavery in America. Each generation relived trauma in their own way—and either broke through on some level, or repeated cycles of abuse and trauma. Each generation also passed down the same trauma-laced genes, whether slightly improved or worsened, for about seven generations, according to Wolynn.

This, for me, meant that every single step that I take towards healing myself will heal my daughters. My pursuit grew with the realization that I will have generations of children standing on my shoulders.

I decided that I would be the one to give them a more solid foundation. I would do the hard work and find a way to heal more fully. In fact, following my alma mater Clark Atlanta University's motto that stuck with me so strongly, I decided that I would "find a way or make one." To date, I am finding many ways that have worked for others, and creating my very own from the mix. You can do this, too.

We heal in cycles

People often think that healing is a single process. It is in fact a continuous process—with a circle of stages that repeats. My healing process had started with counseling in college. I sat with the university counselor once each week—and I suppressed most of my true feelings. I told half-truths and sat quietly much of the time. It was precious time and support, not received in full. I never told the whole truth about my relationship with Ms. Kathy. That might have saved me a lot of grief going forward. I protected her and most of the other abusers in my life. I thought silence was my best option at the time.

Young people often think they know what's best. But knowing is hard to come by without experience turned to wisdom. People will have various experiences that are generally universal. Nobody is as unique as they think. We all have an immense source of power within our human mind and soul. Not everyone takes those experiences and extracts the lessons presented. If we *don't* get the lesson, then we repeat the experience with a different location or face. If we *do* get the lesson, we must now decide how to interpret it and define it for ourselves.

The way we define what we've learned will play a large role in how we feel about it. We must begin to live out loud. I mean we must speak the truth of our circumstances so that we are clear about what we're dealing with. By not speaking the truth to my counselor, I set my healing back in a big way. I was gathering tools from her and others, and using them in secret. Since I had no experience with those tools I wasn't using them effectively. I was also using them based on lies and half-truths.

It was impossible for me to tell lies and half-truths to others for years without believing some of them myself. When we lie to ourselves, we are officially set up to fail. We must face the current truth just as it is—and not try to make the situation seem better or worse. Our emotions are indicators of what could be going on, but they do not dictate what is true. It is helpful to be able to trace an emotion to the source—that is, to place meaning upon an experience. If we

OUR EMOTIONS
ARE INDICATORS
OF WHAT COULD
BE GOING ON,
BUT THEY DO NOT
DICTATE WHAT IS
TRUE.

have chosen to define an experience as something negative or bad, then we will feel negative emotions. The same is true for the opposite. If we have chosen to define an experience as positive, then our positive emotions will follow. Everything in life is always working out for our good. But many of us find that fact hard to believe when unwanted experiences keep showing up.

Turning pain into wisdom

Wisdom comes in as the key that turns knowledge from experiences into Knowing. Wisdom requires that we understand an experience (gather the knowledge) as well as how we viewed it (process the emotions). Then we can make a sound argument for rewriting the story. In this way, it becomes clear that how we defined an experience at the time doesn't matter as much as now knowing what the soul wanted to receive.

The meaning of the story becomes foundational when you want to rewrite that story. You must rewrite your story containing your new, empowering meaning and desired circumstances. When we determine our individual meaning, we take steps in knowing what we truly want to experience going forward—thus creating *a new foundation*. It is then that *we can begin creating new genes and experiences*—and that's when we can fully heal trauma.

It was in my deepest stages of depression and debilitating anxiety that I started to discover a true healing path. I was no longer religious but I knew there was something greater than me in this physical form. I discovered reiki healing, took on a one-on-one teacher, and I learned to meditate.

I went back to counseling while enduring the worst custody fight of my life. This time around in therapy I didn't hide my trauma. I told the truth. Revealing my truth gave my therapist and me the opportunity to choose the right tools and then to put them to proper use. I discovered Abraham Hicks, Joe Dispenza, and many other thought leaders on the Law of Attraction, heart coherence, and innate healing modalities. I studied day and night with YouTube videos, books, meditations—and even hypnotherapies to reach my subconscious while I slept at night. I was fighting for my life.

After some time, I completely stopped fighting with others. Even the one person I thought I should keep fighting with only caused anxiety and other symptoms of PTSD, so I reluctantly let that go, too. I gave up the fight and felt one thousand percent better, knowing that I would return stronger with more resolve. The more I learned, the more I could see the mistakes I had made.

Self-love and self-care

I saw that the answer was to mother myself back to health. I saw that I needed to learn to truly love myself through it all. *Real* self-love!

Many people hear *self-love*, and they think of self-care. *Self-care* is when you take time for yourself. People often demonstrate this with healthy meals, workout regimens, a bath, a manicure, or play time. Self-care is very important in connecting with our physical selves and taking care of our mind and body.

Self-love goes much deeper. Truly loving anything or anyone, and even loving yourself, requires a great deal of knowledge about that thing or that person. So, to love yourself you must know who you truly are. Knowing yourself requires time with yourself. You must be able to sit with yourself—in your pain, confusion, clarity, and bliss, and understand *all* aspects of you.

I had to reach the point where I knew the good, the bad, and the ugly aspects of myself; then I could connect to each aspect with acceptance and compassion. It is then that you'll be able to sincerely declare that you have self-love. Self-love doesn't happen overnight. Just as love grows with others, self-love grows as you learn more about yourself and *respond with loving acceptance.* Therefore, the key to self-love is not only knowing but also accepting yourself for who you are.

You can love your children to the moon and back, but if they don't feel completely accepted in just one area then they will believe your love is limited. We know that love is often limited in some way; but *agape* love—unconditional love—is what we're reaching for with ourselves. It is this *God-level love* that instantly frees us from trauma, PTSD, abuse, codependency, and all other ways of devaluing ourselves.

I didn't get there right away. It was a continuous process with steady progress—which eventually helped me to break through. You will soon see my last biggest test in self-love was rooted in opening my eyes to my codependent ways. Before we get there, allow me to share some of my most impactful practices that have helped me to harness my own power to heal. I know from personal experience that these five practices will guide and benefit you, too:

Five daily practices for successful healing

1. **Protect your mind.**
   - For me, this meant I had to stop watching the news, and instead input as much positivity as possible into my brain. I watched comedy, read and listened to books that were uplifting, and listened to countless gurus and master teachers share wisdom via lectures and courses.

2. **Drink water and move your body.**
   - When you are depressed and unsure of where life is heading, it is easy to want to sit or sleep all day. I forced myself to move my body daily—for most of the day. Sometimes it was going to the gym; other times it was taking advantage of my active job, playing with my toddler, playing with other people's dogs, or even cleaning more slowly just to spread it out.
   - On my most depressed days, I would drink lots of water knowing I would go to the bathroom often, requiring me to at least get up and walk. I would also take advantage of my disgust for clutter, and get up every hour to do one or two tasks that helped to clear my space. After a few days—or sometimes mere hours—I was in a clean, clear space, well hydrated, and I had effectively moved my body for at least one hour each day.

3.   Consciously remove distractions.

- Distractions are more than a notion if you want some time alone with yourself. I would make the decision to turn off all distractions for a certain period of time every day. I started with just ten minutes, and grew it from there. I would take advantage of waiting periods in doctor's offices or restaurants to sit quietly with my thoughts—instead of surfing the net, texting, or even reading a book. I wasn't very good at meditating early on, so sitting quietly was the next best thing.

- I learned a lot about myself. I especially learned about how I think—how I repeat experiences over and over in my mind and how I had a difficult time swiping them away. I learned what my automatic negative thoughts looked like, and when they popped up the most. I learned my triggers and how my mind and body reacted to them. Being quiet and *paying attention to me* was the best thing I could've done to get to know my true self.

4.   Feel it!

- A large part of allowing constant distractions is so that we don't have to pay attention to the upsetting parts of our world. We can use distractions to avoid feeling pain, disappointment, or loss. Even when sitting in silence, many people can still focus on something that creates a distraction from actually feeling. But it is important for us to feel our emotions on the inside. We often spew them out towards others but still don't take the time to feel our emotions within. Taking the time to feel our own emotions will lead us down a path of understanding, and then to acceptance.

5. **Heal fragmentation.**

- As we feel our emotions more and more, we eventually realize the parts of us that aren't feeling loved and accepted. These are our fragmented parts. When we are fragmented or broken inside, we cannot master self-love nor can we heal fully.

- Recognizing our broken parts comes in time. Once recognized, we can heal them quickly. Feeling the emotions and hearing the story of each broken part of ourselves creates a powerful opportunity to mend. When we take the last step *to accept that fragmented self with loving empathy*, then we can be whole again. This is true lasting healing.

There were many hours of learning—trial and error, and even complete failure—as I did everything in my power to heal. These five practices were foundational to my success. I continue to use these practices to maintain my healthy, happy state. If you sincerely do the same and don't give up, they will work for you, too.

Chapter Eight

Codependency-Infused Love

When you try to bring someone along who isn't coming, you hold yourself back, and so you don't go, either.
—Abraham Hicks

Codependence is the most common of all addictions—the addiction to looking elsewhere. We believe that something outside of ourselves—that is, outside of our true self—can give us happiness and fulfillment. The "elsewhere" may be people, places, things, or behaviors and experiences. Whatever it is, we may neglect our own selves for it.
—Charles L. Whitfield, MD

Codependency as a response to trauma

Until late summer, 2016 was turning out to be the most devastating year of my life. At the same time, however, I found myself elevating like never before. I had become proficient at meditation, affirmations, and self-discipline. In many ways, I had also gone from a person who was often indecisive to someone who made solid decisions and took action. I had recently lost the dirtiest custody battle—worse than I could have ever imagined, if not for the direct experience—and found myself with significantly less time with my daughter.

I failed to see the truth of the situation. I didn't know what a narcissist was at the time. I thought Josh had limits—that he would surely stop a false attack if it meant hurting his child. I was wrong. I was caught up in overcompensating for the mothering I did not receive as a child, and I was not paying attention to the reality of my own abuse at the time. I made my child into my entire world and overprotected her.

What was I to do with my life now? Being a new mother was all-consuming and in many ways felt amazing. I now felt that motherhood had been stripped from me. I spiraled into a deep depression.

This process had started months before that, so I had the opportunity to turn to my self-help guides in an effort to push myself through the difficult times. Although dying inside by a million tiny cuts to my self-esteem and my self-worth as a mother, and harboring an overall fear of losing my mind, I put on a brave face and went out into the world. I went to work, I hung out with my friends, and I did a special project for myself. My cousin and my friends had been the best support system a girl could ever ask for during the year before, when Josh put us out of his house. They showed up for me in every way.

I had changed a lot—dealing with the natural hormones of having a baby, PTSD, depression, and then changing my diet and thus my whole way of living altogether. My girlfriends still showed up for me. They made me smile, laugh, and go outside; they celebrated my birthday, and my baby's birthday, and so much more. I count them as a large part of how I survived the extreme changes in my life at that time.

Things got way more complicated in my life as an unexpected war was waged on me and on my very idea of motherhood. I had no idea the enemy had been lying in wait to make me pay for some unknown offense. I wasn't prepared at all, so I lost. I felt so much shame and guilt around the whole experience that I receded into my shell and prayed it would all go away. On the days when I could get out of bed, I went about the day as normally as possible. I made discipline even more important, as that was the only way I knew how to stick to the processes I had learned the year before. I would meditate, recite affirmations, and research my truths in order to reinforce my sanity and to physically get to work. I worked my day job, started working out at a new gym, and found a small home to refurbish. These things kept me very busy so I could actually be interested in something other than my daughter.

When my daughter was with me, everything came easily. My energy was as high as my spirits when she was around. There was no dragging myself out of bed at all; instead, I would awaken at 5:00 a.m., knowing she would wobble into my room at any moment and climb into the bed with me.

Life was starting to take shape again as I learned to more effectively wall off my feelings. I reveled in the presence of my child and otherwise numbed myself with activity and enough alcohol to help me sleep at night. The funny thing is, I actually thought I was doing well, considering the circumstances. I would often think to myself, "God is funny...tricky even," because I was sure that I would've put myself out of my misery if I didn't have my child to live for. That being said, I wouldn't have been experiencing that level of misery in the first place if I didn't have this child. It rings of the funny but sad cliché of "stuck between a rock and a hard place."

I reminded myself daily of how much better off I was because I'd brought this child into the world. I believe in destiny—that everything happens for a reason. Whether that reason is wanted or understood is another thing—of which, I've learned that it doesn't really matter. I reminded myself daily as I listened to recordings of Abraham Hicks explain how life works: "Everything is always working out for me."

I moved into my newly renovated house with reignited confidence and happiness that summer. My daily practices became easier and I began to record in my journal my emotions, thoughts, and beliefs. In addition to my self-care, I began to reach out to the world on Facebook to talk about my experiences and how I had gotten through things so far. I felt accomplished in many ways as I wavered day by day— sitting in my misery, and then pushing through it.

I was mostly distracted by my life but I still felt one thing was missing. I wanted a lover. I wanted a partner to talk to and hang out with and be intimate with. I knew I had a way to go in my healing journey but I felt like my active work in that area had made me ready for a relationship. In particular, I wanted a girlfriend. I had been practicing visualization for the past several months. On some subjects it felt easy but it felt very difficult on others. One lonely Saturday afternoon I decided to give it a try and envision myself having a beautiful girlfriend who was fun and sexy.

My girlfriend showed up three weeks later. I had already met her a couple of months before I did my visualization but I hadn't looked at her as a potential mate. She stopped me on my way out of a social gathering that day and asked to stay connected. We exchanged information and she had already reached out a few times asking if I wanted to attend an event with her or have lunch. I still didn't think that she was hitting on me but just that she wanted a friend. Her advances always fell on a day when I had my daughter so I turned her down each time. The last time I turned her down I explained my schedule and gave her the next weekend I would be available with advance notice. She asked to get on my calendar for that open weekend for brunch and we finally met again.

I sat in the bar area of the winery, comfortable in the half-wrinkled jeans dress and croc sandals I had thrown on. I wasn't sure if I really remembered how she looked and if I would recognize her easily. I sat facing the entrance, thinking it would give me time to do a facial recognition scan in between glances at the menu.

I noticed her immediately as she rounded the corner into the bar area. She was all dressed up by my standards—in a tight-fitting skirt and tank top, and wearing what I called real shoes. Those were any shoes other than flip-flops or gym shoes. Now I noticed her. I saw how sexy she was and her smile topped it off. I stood to hug her as she approached me with open arms. That was when I finally realized that she wanted to be more than just friends.

I smiled broadly. "Yvette, you look great. I thought you were coming straight from the gym."

She laughed. "I did just come from the gym. I taught a class this morning, and then showered and changed."

I was impressed. I hated taking real clothes to the gym to change into after a workout. I did it often enough when I had to go straight to work afterwards but it felt like a huge chore and not worth the time and effort.

Yvette spoke to every staff member in the bar area as she got comfortable in her seat. She was clearly a regular at the winery. Conversation flowed easily as we chatted about our work and lives in general. We laughed and gazed into each other's eyes and generally enjoyed talking to each other. It felt like we talked for hours. We actually had talked for at least two hours, as that is the amount of time I had allotted for our lunch before my furniture delivery window started. Since I had only recently moved into my new home, I didn't have any living room furniture so my couch was being delivered that day.

I saw calls come in back to back and finally paid attention to the time. I answered the next call thinking it might be the couch delivery, and it was. They were leaving my house because nobody was home. I argued that they were early and not within my delivery window so it would only be fair if they came back an hour later. Surprisingly, they agreed.

I explained to Yvette that I had a furniture delivery

coming and hadn't planned on lunch going on so long. We were halfway through our second bottle of wine and I felt very comfortable with her so I invited her to my house to continue chatting and drinking wine.

She smirked and asked if it was a ploy to get her back to my place.

I answered no, but I said I would like it if she'd come over and continue hanging out.

She agreed with a sly look that made me want to kiss her lips. Instead, I texted her my address and asked for the check.

Yvette followed me into my driveway minutes later. She got out and exclaimed, "We live so close!" She said her house was less than a mile away from mine.

We went inside and continued our conversation and drinking at my kitchen island. I didn't have a huge tolerance for alcohol so I was already feeling quite buzzed. Our conversation deepened as we asked more personal questions and told our individual haunted stories about relationships. While I had escaped an abusive one in some ways, and in other ways I was still dealing with that abuse, Yvette was at the tail end of a marriage gone bad. We both had deep pain rooted in betrayal and abandonment. We felt closer with each spoken similarity, along with each additional sip of wine.

Finally, I looked at the clock and noticed the furniture company had not returned with my couch. I called to complain and they rescheduled my delivery.

Yvette teased me, saying that there was never really a furniture delivery—that it was me simply trying to get her into my house. She asked over and over again as she put her face in mine, "Why did you want me to come over?"

I blushed and denied her accusation. She was so close I could feel the heat radiating from her entire body. I leaned in until our lips were barely touching and whispered, "What if there really were a plan to get you here?"

She smiled and kissed me. As we broke apart she complained that she had been in my house for hours and I hadn't even given her a tour.

I chuckled. "The house is so small you can see the whole thing from here."

"No, there are doors closed back there," she argued.

I jumped down from the bar stool and took her hand. I led her to the back where I opened the bathroom door, my daughter's room door, and finally my bedroom door.

She stepped into my bedroom pulling me in with her, and promptly pushed me down onto the bed. We had an intense passionate experience as if we'd known each other for years. It was then that our trauma bond was sealed.

Trauma bonding

Codependency is an emotional and behavioral condition that is often referred to as relationship addiction. It is very common between two people who have experienced trauma. Trauma bonding creates a most powerful and intense codependent relationship. These relationships are often one-sided, emotionally destructive, or even abusive.

Patrick Carnes, a professional counselor, put forth the idea that some sexual behavior is an addiction. Carnes created the International Institute for Trauma and Addiction Professionals

(IITAP) where he taught about trauma bonding and much more. When a person has ongoing cycles of abuse, the rewards and punishments in a relationship come in random unexpected intervals. This creates excitement, fear, and sexual feelings that entangle a person in powerful emotional bonds that are difficult to change. Bonding is a biological response to these intense emotions. These codependent bonds are often mistaken for healthy relationships despite the pain and trauma involved in them. People tend to think that intense emotion means something positive within a relationship, when in fact, intense emotion can come from pain *or* pleasure.

I had done this before. I had endured codependent relationships without knowing what they were—my biggest one being with Ms. Kathy. This time it was like having an out-of-body experience. I could see myself making the same mistakes and I knew better—but somehow I couldn't stop myself. I practiced the things I learned every day and didn't get discouraged—even though I knew I was sometimes still making bad decisions for myself.

There was something in me that called me to this person regardless of what she did. Was that the unconditional love that I had been searching for? I practiced and practiced loving entirely without expecting anything specific in return. I continued to study, and learned that the struggle I felt was between me and me—that is, between my physical self and my inner being or higher self. I felt the struggle but also profoundly felt the love. As I learned more about myself on a deeper level, I realized that *I* was the one in need of unconditional love. If I couldn't *love myself* on that level, there was no way I could love someone else that way and have it returned. I had to reconnect with *me*.

Eventually Yvette had to be moved out of my experience, since we weren't on the same wavelength. But I didn't let go as soon as I should have. This only prolonged the inevitable and deepened the pain.

Learning lessons in the cycle of enlightenment

When is the last time you held on too long? What excuses did you use to prolong the inevitable? What emotions did you feel while holding on?

A codependent relationship shows up to reveal where you are in your healing. There's something to be said about the cycle of enlightenment. We think we are moving in a linear direction only to find, through experience—deemed good or bad—that the path is indeed spiraled. We end up right where we were before, looking at the same obstacle or pain or triumph, but from a different level. That level can be higher, lower, or even the same, depending on where we are in the healing cycle.

If you are repeating a cycle, then you have yet to learn the lessons. I clearly had not fully learned the self-love lesson. Yet I had made lots of progress and could see my mistakes, and thus I could see how to move forward.

It is immensely important that you see yourself, your missteps, your problems, and your life developments as they truly are. Make a real effort not to see things as worse than they are because you will only damage any progress you've made. You must also not see things as better than they truly

AS A PERSON WHO'S EXPERIENCED TRAUMA, I KNOW THAT IT IS DANGEROUS TO PRETEND THAT YOU ARE HEALED WHEN YOU ARE NOT.

are, for danger of tricking yourself into thinking you've made progress when you really haven't.

As a person who's experienced trauma, I know that it is dangerous to pretend that you are healed when you are not. Pretending will land you in another abusive situation, perhaps even worse than any you've had before. Choose to see the truth of your life and face situations as they are in the present. That is the only way you can set realistic goals and move forward.

Chapter Nine

I Am Lorraine

My mom gave me the middle name Lorraine after an aunt who died before I was born. As the story goes, she was married to a man whom she loved enormously. He was her whole life and she took pride and joy in loving him with her whole heart. But he left her—for God knows who or what—and it broke her heart. She drank and drank, and ultimately died from what my mom calls a broken heart.

When I was a little girl, I thought she literally died from a broken heart. I didn't realize she had drunk herself to death. Lorraine died from cirrhosis of the liver because she drank her sorrow away. She had the biggest heartbreak of her life and didn't know how to handle it, so she essentially died from it.

Why would my mom name me after someone like that? I hated my name for years because of that story. I did not understand how, as a young person at the time, Mom admired someone who would kill herself over love lost. I didn't understand how seeing me as just a baby, she would give me a name with a story that meant that I could feel that intensely. So

I just didn't like my name and didn't tell anyone if I didn't have to—until I got a little older and I decided to ask her why she named me after my Aunt Lorraine.

Mom explained that Lorraine had very intense feelings, and she really did break down from a broken heart and drink herself to death. But she also explained that Lorraine had the brightest smile she had ever seen. Mom said that Lorraine was the kindest woman anybody had ever known: She would help anybody she could and she always knew the right things to say to help people feel better. She was wise beyond her years and didn't let anyone tell her that she didn't know what she was doing. Lorraine felt deeply, and made no apologies for that. Even when she drank herself into a stupor, she never apologized for feeling her feelings. My Aunt Lorraine was someone people looked up to, and people loved to be around her. She was also someone most people didn't quite understand. But no one could deny how special she was.

That explanation resonated with me completely. I can understand how a person can exist in such duality. I often felt like I had a few of my own personalities, all dueling to get to the top. In one moment I wanted to fight for revenge and fairness via any means necessary. In another moment I wanted to take a peaceful stance in every area of my life. This was true even when someone was blatantly taking advantage of me or deliberately trying to hurt me.

The Self-Mothering effect

I asked the question over and over again: "Who am I?"

For reasons I couldn't explain, I took names seriously. I feel there is some direction in them. My first name, Crescenda, means "steady rising" so I knew that although I started off with a lowly life, my life could only get better from there. My middle name confused me for a long time but after years of internal fighting with pain and grief, feeling alone and too different, I finally began to see a different point of view. I now saw my Aunt Lorraine's intensity as a gift instead of a curse. Her intense ability to love and to show emotion was the beginning of a profound healing journey that every woman in my family needed. Many found her intensity a weak trait and vowed to never be that weak themselves. With that decision, when it came to love, unfortunately they took more care to never fully commit to others, to distrust, and to live fully in survival mode.

We've already discussed how survival mode enacts the fight-or-flight system in our bodies and minds. In this mode, every ounce of energy we have is directed to making sure our physical body and surroundings are safe. Therefore, my family focused on material things and those of an external nature—all the while ignoring real internal feelings, creative ideas, and long-term or love-based desires.

Since survival mode is toxic in the long run, it leaves no room for a healthy family or for loving relationships. These things require us to relax and digest our truths beyond the physical. My Aunt Lorraine chose to give attention to her parasympathetic nervous system—that is, she allowed her feelings to be felt. Maybe she was the first woman in a long line of women in our family who had done this in decades.

Maybe she simply couldn't find a balance because it was so new to her and she had no role models to follow.

Maybe Lorraine laid the foundation, however rocky, for the next generation to balance and solidify. I didn't notice anyone in my mother's generation take up the work of shutting down our survival mode as the main mode of reacting so that we could find a balance in our hormonal responses. Maybe someone did try but found it too difficult to carry on.

Now that I can see a different way and feel the need so clearly, I realize that it must be my turn to take up the torch and teach as a living example that *we can thrive outside of survival mode*. In fact, cultivating balance is the only way we can not only survive but truly thrive—and correct and create healthy families and loving relationships along the way.

If it's up to me, I must re-establish the importance of motherhood. Not literally having more children and being a mother—but I'm talking about that mothering quality: the nurturing, loving directional push that every person, young and old, needs. My mother clearly needed some mothering, and when she didn't get it, she had to develop the skills to mother herself into health, clarity, and balance. I don't know that she would consider herself healed but I hope Mom is at least in a space of radical acceptance of herself. Regardless of my mother's journey, my self-love and healing have led me to an acceptance of my mom and of my upbringing. I now know that she truly did the best that she could do while living in survival mode. I now have an enormous amount of compassion for my mom and appreciate her contribution to our family's healing journey. I now see her heart and soul—and it is golden.

I want to be the mother who can give these self-mothering skills to my children as I show them how to be a nurturing parent. I wonder about the world and what it would be like if more women knew how to mother themselves as well as their children. Wouldn't we be a more balanced society? Wouldn't we be a healthier people overall, because we've taken the time to do the hard work of healing ourselves first?

I've talked about the vital importance of *forgiveness* for so many years—but what if it's not about forgiveness at all? What if I simply needed to *understand* my foremothers' lives more, and in the process to discover my own purpose?

Now that I understand more, I don't feel the need to forgive. I appreciate every step of the journey that let me know with no uncertainty that I need to learn unconditional love and apply it liberally. My Aunt Lorraine would have benefitted greatly from a more balanced kind of unconditional love—which included herself. She loved another person unconditionally but couldn't turn that love inward to save her own life.

I now know that saving my own life *first* is the way that I can live and walk in unconditional love for others. If I can truly heal me, then I can accept others for who they are, and not take their desires and ideals personally. The power that I feel knowing that I can take control of my feelings and be in charge of my own healing is too much for words. I can literally heal myself out of huge bouts of depression. I can heal myself out of my past traumatic experiences. I can heal myself out of pain and away from triggers of mother–daughter relationships gone awry. I can heal myself out of the need to analyze, rationalize, and forgive the people I loved but who chose to focus elsewhere.

I can truly mother myself into healing so that I can feel whatever I'm feeling, yet still have balance in clarity, perspective, and complete love—regardless of how it appears to others. Maybe I was made to love intensely so that others can see and know that it is possible to do so in a healthy and safe way. I dare to see this journey through.

Your own self-mothering journey has begun. Know that you are not alone. Your success is certain, if you remember that it is all about unconditional love for yourself. You now know that you can heal yourself—without drugs, years of therapy, or hypnosis. You can heal fully and faster with the WAAKE Healing Methodology.

Don't delay. Put the WAAKE healing method to the test in your own life and witness your own trauma transform to power. As you begin to see the new you, there might be the temptation to waver back to your old set point—but remember: It is the self-mothering effect that helps to see you through.

Mother yourself to health. Be patient, nurturing, and kind to yourself as you journey through your healing process. You've got this!

Book Club Discussion Guide

Ask yourself these questions as you write in your journal:

1. How do you recognize your own survival mode?
2. Which of the six tenets of survival mode resonate with you the most? (See Chapter Three, p. 43.)
3. Write out your main pivotal story for yourself. Which tenets of survival mode can you identify in this story?
4. How do those tenets play out in your life right now?
5. Which tenet of survival mode drives you the most?

As you continue your journaling journey, ask yourself these questions to assess your own WAAKE (Wiring, Awareness Assistance, Knowing, and Esteem):

6. What do I believe about myself?
7. What do I believe about other people?
8. Why did I respond with [insert negative emotions] to this pivotal experience [insert specific incident]?
9. Where in my life might I have dealt with a narcissist?
10. Have I been codependent in a relationship? When?

11. Are there events, words, and/or thoughts that trigger me back into [insert the negative experience]? What are they? Write out all the triggers that occur to you.

12. What story do I have that is keeping me stuck?

13. What story represents my truth? Is this story currently serving me in a positive way? Or keeping me stuck?

14. How might I change a trauma-based story into an empowering story? [Retrace my story. See p. 103.]

15. What's one small step that I can take today to begin transforming my trauma into power? *Make answering this question your daily practice.*

Further Reading

Carnes, Patrick. *Don't Call It Love: Recovery from Sexual Addiction.* New York: Bantam Books, 1992. Get a better understanding of trauma bonding with this book.

De Bellis, Michael D., and Abigail Zisk. "The Biological Effects of Childhood Trauma." *Child and Adolescent Psychiatric Clinics of North America*, vol. 23, no. 2, 2014, p. 185–222, doi:10.1016/j.chc.2014.01.002. A deep dive into generational trauma patterns and how to gain better awareness of what's passed down in our genes.

Dutton, Painter. "Traumatic Bonding: The Development of Emotional Attachments in Battered Women and Other Relationships of Intermittent Abuse." *Victimology: An International Journal* (7), 1981. A deep dive into trauma bonding and codependency.

Felitti, Vincent J., et al. Reprint: "Relationship of Childhood Abuse and Household Dysfunction to Many of the Leading Causes of Death in Adults: The Adverse Childhood Experiences (ACEs) Study." *American Journal of Preventive*

Medicine, vol. 56, no. 6, 2019, p. 774–786, doi:10.1016/j. amepre.2019.04.001. A study showing a direct link between childhood abuse or neglect and adult mental and emotional conditions.

Goddard, Neville. "The Pruning Shears of Revision," 1954. Lecture, available from www.imaginationandfaith.com. Understanding our relationship to our Source [or God].

Hicks, Esther. "Abraham-Hicks Publications—Law of Attraction Official Site." *Home of Abraham-Hicks Law of Attraction*, 30 Oct. 2020, www.abraham-hicks.com. Gain a deeper understanding of the Law of Attraction via videos, recordings, and books.

Miller, Joshua D., et al. "Assessment of Personality Disorders and Related Traits: Bridging DSM-IV-TR and DSM-5." *The Oxford Handbook of Personality Disorders*, 2012, p. 107–140, doi:10.1093/oxfordhb/9780199735013.013.0006. Identifying personality disorders based on common traits.

Nunez, Kristen. "Fight, Flight, or Freeze: How We Respond to Threats." 21 Feb. 2020, www.healthline.com/health/mental-health/fight-flight-freeze. Understand the basis of survival mode.

Whitfield, Charles L., and Cardwell C. Nuckols. *Healing the Child Within: Discovery and Recovery for Adult Children of Dysfunctional Families*. Health Communications, 2015. A deeper look at the benefits of nurturing yourself to health.

Wolynn, Mark. *It Didn't Start with You: How Inherited Family Trauma Shapes Who We Are and How to End the Cycle*. New York: Penguin Publishing Group, 2017. How we inherit trauma and perpetuate it through many generations, even in our genes.

Additional Resources

www.acestoohigh.com/got-your-ace-score. Find your Adverse Childhood Experiences (ACEs) score here.

Anna Foundation, www.theannainstitute.org. This website is an education and resource center focusing on the impacts of childhood trauma and paths to prevention and healing.

Beattie, Melody. *Codependent No More: How to Stop Controlling Others and Start Caring for Yourself.* Center City, Minn.: Hazelden Publishing, 2016. First published in 1986, this ground-breaking book is a modern classic.

"Behavioral Health Treatment Services Locator." *Home— SAMHSA Behavioral Health Treatment Services Locator,* www. findtreatment.samhsa.gov. Immediate help and crisis control can be found here.

Byrne, Rhonda. *The Secret.* Miami, Fla.: Atria Books, 2018. A good foundational understanding of the Law of Attraction.

Carnes, Patrick. *Betrayal Bond: Breaking Free of Exploitive Relationships*. Boca Raton, Fla.: Health Communications Incorporated Books, 2019. This is a deep dive into self-love and how it heals our lives and relationships.

Dispenza, Joe. *Breaking the Habit of Being Yourself: How to Lose Your Mind and Create a New One*. Carlsbad, Calif.: Hay House, 2018. A deeper understanding of mind over matter and how we can control our circumstances.

Dispenza, Joe, and Gregg Braden. *Becoming Supernatural: How Common People Are Doing the Uncommon*. Carlsbad, Calif.: Hay House, Inc., 2019.

Hicks, Esther. *Ask and It Is given: an Introduction to the Teachings of Abraham-Hicks*. Carlsbad, Calif.: Hay House Inc, 2011. A comprehensive understanding of the Law of Attraction and our relationship to the universe.

About the Author

With *The Self-Mothering Effect*, Crescenda Bramlett, known to all as LadyWake, adds published author to her list of job titles—which includes healthcare consultant, salesperson, relationship and trauma healing coach, spiritual counselor, reiki professional, fitness instructor, mom, and youth speaker and motivator. As a Trauma Transformation Coach, LadyWake is focused on breaking generational trauma patterns and transforming trauma into power. She has survived multiple layers of abuse and trauma, which has fueled her life's work.

LadyWake has transformed her harmful survival-mode side effects into modes of thriving, with her two daughters as her angelic push. She continues to help women harness their own power to do the same.

About the Author

Contact the Author

Website

www.ladywakett.com

Social Media

Facebook.com/LadyWakeTT

Instagram @iamladywakett

Please Post a Review!

If you like what you read in *The Self-Mothering Effect*, please post a review at your favorite online retailer. This will help me reach more people with this message. Thank you.

Made in the USA
Monee, IL
23 November 2024

71023239R00085